ROBERT
HENRYSON

ROBERT HENRYSON

By

MARSHALL W. Winslow STEARNS

AMS PRESS, INC.
NEW YORK
1966

B
H525s

TO

Edith Winslow Stearns

PREFACE

*P*ROFESSORS W. A. NEILSON AND K. G. T. WEBSTER asserted not long ago that "it is doubtful whether there is in the whole of English literature a case of neglected genius so remarkable as that of Henryson." Whether or not the poet is a genius is a matter of opinion, but that he has been neglected is a matter of fact. He is recognized today, if at all, as the author of the first English pastoral, *Robene and Makyne,* and on the strength of this poem he is included occasionally in anthologies. He is also credited, within academic walls, with the authorship of a sequel to Chaucer's *Troilus and Criseyde.* With the exception of infrequent flashes of approval by some voyager in the realm of forgotten literature, Henryson has received little or no further attention. It may be that the volume of his work appears to be too slight, or the nature of his genius too derivative. The object of the present study is to correct such misconceptions and to clear the way for a better understanding and appreciation of the poet and his poetry.

The author would like to take this opportunity to express his gratitude to Professors Rudolph Gottfried, David Daiches, and B. J. Whiting for their kind help at various stages in the preparation of this book. Nor would the expression of indebtedness be complete without mentioning the invaluable advice and counsel of Professor Karl Young, under whom this study of Henryson was initiated.

Grateful acknowledgment is made to *ELH, A Journal of English Literary History; Modern Philology; Modern Language Notes; Modern Language Quarterly; Publications of the Modern Lan-*

guage Association; Indiana University Publications; and Houghton Mifflin Company, for permission to reprint some of the material included in this book.

M.W.S.

Ithaca, New York
December, 1948

CONTENTS

ROBERT
HENRYSON

Chapter I

THE POETRY AND LIFE OF
ROBERT HENRYSON

*T*HE REPUTATION OF ROBERT HENRYSON is still in the process of being established. Even his own countrymen found little merit in him until comparatively recently and were inclined to prefer other Scottish authors. In 1786 John Pinkerton, an early editor of the older Scottish poetry, announced that he liked Dunbar better than Chaucer but he had nothing to say in favor of Henryson.[1] The first adequate estimate of the poet was made by William Ernest Henley in 1880, in a brief preface to selections from Henryson's works:

Henryson was an accomplished man and a good and genuine poet. He had studied Chaucer with the ardour and insight of an original mind, and while he has much in common with his master, he has much that is his own . . . He narrates with a gaiety, an ease, a rapidity, not to be surpassed in English literature between Chaucer and Burns.[2]

Henley added that "to a modern eye his dialect is distressingly quaint and crabbed," a comment which caused resentment among Scottish scholars.[3]

Recognition of Henryson in the United States was even more delayed. In 1888 James Russell Lowell condemned fifteenth-century Scottish poetry in general and the Middle Scots dialect in particular,[4]

[1] John Pinkerton, ed., *Ancient Scotish Poems*, pp. ix–xi, xciv.
[2] T. H. Ward, ed., *The English Poets*, I, 138. For scattered comments on Henryson before Henley, cf. W. Geddie, *A Bibliography of Middle Scots Poets*, pp. 175 ff.
[3] G. G. Smith, ed., *The Poems of Robert Henryson*, STS, I, xiii and note.
[4] J. R. Lowell, *The English Poets*, p. 13. For an adverse estimate of Lowell's critical ability, cf. Van Wyck Brooks, *The Flowering of New England*, pp. 517 ff.

while four years later T. R. Lounsbury observed that Henryson is "one of those early writers whom Scottish patriotism struggles energetically to consider a poet." [5]

The tide was turning in England, however, and W. W. Skeat, in the course of editing various "Chaucerian" poems in 1897, spoke of the *Testament of Cresseid* as perhaps the "best piece" in the volume.[6] In the following year, George Saintsbury remarked of Henryson's poems: "The total bulk is not large, but the merit is, for the fifteenth century more particularly, very high, and the variety of directions in which it is shown is extremely remarkable." Saintsbury selected two passages in the *Testament of Cresseid* for comment: "The two great passages of the doom of Saturn and the meeting would of itself [*sic*] give this poem rank with, if not above, the best work of the century, but the whole is not unworthy of them." [7]

Adequate recognition of Henryson's accomplishment and of the unwarranted obscurity in which his poetry had long existed occurred in 1916, when W. A. Neilson and K. G. T. Webster edited at Harvard a volume of fourteenth- and fifteenth-century poetry. It is significant that the editors felt it necessary to devote an entire paragraph of their one-page preface to an explanation of why Middle Scots poetry was included in their anthology:

A notable feature of the collection is the prominence given to the Scottish poets of the period. Partly on account of the political separation of England and Scotland, partly through an exaggerated sense of the difficulty of the dialect, students of English literature have unduly neglected these writers. Yet after a few peculiarities in spelling have been noted, Barbour, for example, is as easy as Chaucer; and in the matter of poetic quality none of Chaucer's English disciples is the equal of Henryson or Dunbar. The latter, it is true, is often mentioned if seldom read; but it is doubtful whether there is in the whole of English literature a case of neglected

---

[5] T. R. Lounsbury, *Studies in Chaucer*, I, 459.
[6] W. W. Skeat, *Chaucerian and Other Pieces*, p. lvii.
[7] G. Saintsbury, *A Short History of English Literature*, p. 184.

genius so remarkable as that of Henryson. This book will justify itself if it does no more than make accessible and call attention to poetry of so much interest and distinction.[8]

In the notes, the editors comment further on Henryson:

His *Testament of Cresseid,* written mostly in Chaucer's seven-line stanza, is, although a bit laden with mediaeval machinery at the start, one of the most powerful and affecting poems of the century, as his *Robyn and Makyn* is one of the most graceful and pleasing of the pastorals. The thirteen *Fables* are perhaps an even more significant accomplishment, for to this time-honored theme Henryson has brought so much vivacity and acute, sympathetic observation of men and beasts, that no fables have more flavor than his.[9]

Although no separate study of Henryson has been made up to the present, the poet has met with passing approval from an increasing number of sources.

More recently, Arthur Quiller-Couch praised the Scottish Chaucerians, referring to Henryson as "the manliest, most original of them all," and asserting that the *Testament of Cresseid* is a "noble, passionate poem, and (I dare say) touched with the true fire of the masterpiece for which it was written as a sequel." [10] Aldous Huxley remarks that the same poem is outstanding and that "of all the disciples of Chaucer, from Hoccleve and the Monk of Bury to Mr. Masefield, Henryson may deservedly claim to stand the highest." [11] H. J. C. Grierson speaks of the poem as "perhaps the most original poem that Scotland has produced," [12] while G. G. Coulton feels that it is the "best of all poems in the post-Chaucerian school." [13] Such comments

---

[8] W. A. Neilson and K. G. T. Webster, eds., *Chief British Poets of the Fourteenth and Fifteenth Centuries,* Preface (unpaged). Reprinted by permission of Houghton Mifflin Company.

[9] *Ibid.,* p. 434.

[10] A. Quiller-Couch, *Studies in Literature,* Second Series, II, 269–71.

[11] Aldous Huxley, *Essays New and Old,* p. 272.

[12] H. J. C. Grierson, *The Modern Scot,* IV, 299.

[13] G. G. Coulton, *Medieval Panorama,* p. 589.

could be multiplied freely,[14] and accordingly Henryson's reputation seems virtually secure.

I

Henryson's poetry is perhaps the best of a sudden and transitory literature which flowered in Scotland during the last half of the fifteenth and the beginning of the sixteenth centuries. Alliterative verse of a more popular nature existed before, during, and after this flowering, but for nearly two centuries it was subordinated to a new poetry inspired largely by Chaucer. The new poetry was written in Middle Scots, a literary language which was probably never spoken.[15] If the credit for pioneering belongs to James I (1394–1437), who wrote the *Kingis Quair* in acknowledged imitation of Chaucer, the honor of having mastered the new medium belongs to Robert Henryson, whose *Testament of Cresseid* has the distinction of being a truly successful sequel and whose poetry far surpasses the poetry of Chaucer's English imitators.

Henryson was followed by William Dunbar and Gawin Douglas, who completed the flowering in a manner perhaps less Chaucerian. For although all four poets have been justly called "Scottish Chaucerians," James I, and to a lesser degree Dunbar and Douglas, admired Chaucer chiefly for his mastery of the new allegorical style with its appropriate colors of rhetoric, tending to imitate the poet of the dream-visions and the translator of the *Roman de la Rose*, while Henryson, the only Scottish Chaucerian who was not a court poet,

[14] Cf. G. Bullett, "The Fortunes of Cressida," *New Statesman*, XXI (1923), 361–63; J. M. Manley, *Some New Light on Chaucer*, pp. 289–90; W. P. Ker, *Form and Style in Poetry*, pp. 85–87; G. P. Krapp, *Troilus and Cressida*, p. 16; R. K. Gordon, *The Story of Troilus*, p. xvii; W. Power, *Literature and Oatmeal*, p. 47; M. M. Gray, ed., *Scottish Poetry*, p. ix; J. Speirs, *The Scots Literary Tradition*, pp. 11 ff.; G. Tillotson, *Essays*, pp. 1–4; Marianne Moore, "Feeling and Precision," *Sewanee Review*, LII (1944), 503. I regret that I was unable to see E. M. W. Tillyard's *Five Poems 1470–1870* (London, 1948) before going to press.

[15] Cf. H. H. Wood, ed., *The Poems and Fables of Robert Henryson*, pp. xxxi–xxxiv.

was inclined toward the living rather than the formal aspects of Chaucer's allegory and reproduced more faithfully the spirit of his master.[16]

The canon of Henryson's works is reasonably well defined: three long and thirteen short poems.[17] Opinion is divided as to whether the *Testament of Cresseid* or the *Moral Fables of Aesop* is his best poem; both works are derivative and original at the same time (therein lies the paradox of an author who makes his borrowings his own). In the *Testament,* Henryson, like Chaucer, expresses a strong, sincere, and personal sympathy for his heroine, but the mood of the Scottish poem is one of stern pity and Cresseid's fate is described with the tragic directness of a ballad.[18] The *Fables* consist of thirteen vivid stories which are told as if for the first time.[19] Perhaps the poet's most characteristic achievement here is his success in walking the shadowy line between mice and men, blending fantasy with fact without destroying the illusion of reality. Although they are comic rather than tragic, the *Fables* have the same broad humanity which may be found in the *Testament* and the work of Chaucer.

Henryson's third long poem, the *Orpheus and Eurydice,* is inferior to the *Testament* and the *Fables,* but the charming complaint of Orpheus, with its singing refrain, has an impressive elegiac quality.[20] Of the thirteen minor poems, two deserve separate mention. The

---

[16] Cf. J. M. Smith, *The French Background of Middle Scots Literature,* pp. xvi–xvii.

[17] There is a lost poem, and a few minor pieces have been ascribed to Henryson on insufficient grounds. See G. G. Smith, ed., *The Poems of Robert Henryson,* I, xxvii ff.

[18] There are no early manuscripts of the *Testament,* but an excellent and unique text, printed by Henry Charteris in 1593, is preserved in the British Museum. Cf. H. H. Wood, ed., *Poems and Fables of . . . Henryson,* pp. xxv–xxvi. A list of manuscript and printed texts of the *Testament* is given in Appendix A. For the date of the *Testament,* cf. B. J. Whiting's penetrating article, "A Probable Allusion to Henryson's *Testament of Cresseid,*" *Modern Language Review,* XL (January, 1945), 46–47.

[19] The best discussion of texts of the *Fables* occurs in H. H. Wood, ed., *Poems and Fables of . . . Henryson,* pp. xix–xxiv; the sources are ably examined by G. G. Smith, ed., *Poems of . . . Henryson,* I, xxix–xlv.

[20] For a discussion of texts and sources, cf. H. H. Wood, ed., *Poems and Fables of*

pastoral, *Robene and Makyne,* which shows no Chaucerian influence
and for which no likely model has been found among the extant
pastourelles,[21] far surpasses its later analogue, *The Nut Brown Maid.*
Makyne, portrayed with spirit, appears to be original, and her frank-
ness (for it is she who says, "The man that will nocht quhen he
may sall haif nocht quhen he wald") is the poet's invention. Again,
Henryson's *Sum Practysis of Medecyne* is a riotous satire on the
medical profession, reminiscent, as Gregory Smith says, of Lewis
Carroll's *Hunting of the Snark.* Written with great technical power,
this poem is the poet's only essay in popular alliterative verse.[22] With
the exception of the *Testament,* none of these poems may be said to
have had much influence in succeeding ages.[23]

II

The material for a biography of Robert Henryson is almost negligible. The place of his birth is unknown; authentic details of his
career are altogether lacking; and no single date in his life can be
established with certainty. The approximate dates c. 1425–c. 1506
represent the consensus of opinion. Yet there is proof that he flourished
in Scotland during the latter half of the fifteenth century, and there is
a certain amount of plausible evidence concerning his occupation and
place of residence.

There are four pertinent references to Henryson in the literature
of his times; all of them occur after the probable date of his death.
In his *Lament for the Makaris,* printed by Chepman and Myllar
about 1508,[24] Dunbar speaks of Death (ll. 81–82):

. . . *Henryson,* pp. xxvi–xxvii, and G. G. Smith, ed., *Poems of . . . Henryson,* I,
xlix–lv.

[21] Cf. J. M. Smith, *op. cit.,* pp. 42–46. Cf. further, W. P. Jones, "A Source for
Henryson's *Robene and Makyne?" MLN,* XLVI (November, 1931), 457.

[22] For an analysis of Henryson's metrical skill, cf. G. Saintsbury, *History of English Prosody,* I, 271–72.

[23] Cf. G. G. Smith, ed., *Poems of . . . Henryson,* I, xci ff., where borrowings by
Douglas, Montgomerie, Lyndsay, Wyatt, and others are suggested.

[24] The *Lament* itself is undated, but it is found in a tract entitled *The Porteous of*

In Dunfermelyne he has done rovne
With Maister robert henrisoun.

This reference, which fixes a posterior limit to the poet's life, is supplemented by a reference in David Lyndsay's *Testament and Complaynt of our Soverane Lordis Papyngo,* printed in 1538, which lists the poets then dead, including Henryson.[25] Again, a reference by Gawin Douglas to the poet's *Orpheus and Eurydice* occurs in a holograph gloss to the word "muse," in Douglas' translation of the *Aeneid* (c. 1522):

Musa in Grew signifeis an inventryce or invention in our langgage. And of the ix Musis sum thing in my palys of honour and be Mastir robert hendirson in new orpheus.[26]

The most detailed reference to Henryson, however, occurs in Francis Kinaston's Latin translation of *Troilus and Criseyde,* made about 1639; Kinaston adds a Latin version of the *Testament of Cresseid,* introduced by the following note:

For the Author of this supplement called the Testament of Creseid, which may passe for the sixt & laste booke of this story I haue very sufficiently bin informed by Sr Tho: [27] Eriskin late earle of Kelly & diuers aged schollers of the Scottish nation, that it was made & written by one Mr Robert Henderson sometimes cheife schoolemaster in Dumfermling much about the time that Chaucer was first printed & dedicated to king Henry the 8th by Mr Thinne which was neere the end of his raigne: This Mr Henderson wittily obseruing, that Chaucer in his 5th booke had related the death of Troilus, but made no mention what became of Creseid, he learnedly takes vppon him in a fine poeticall way to expres the punishment & end due to a false vnconstant whore, which commonly terminates in extreme misery, about, or a litle after his time the most famous of the Scottish poets [28]

Noblenes and ten other rare tracts, printed in 1508. Cf. G. G. Smith, ed., *Poems of . . . Henryson,* I, xx.

[25] David Laing, ed., *The Poetical Works of Sir David Lyndsay,* I, 62.

[26] Cambridge MS, Gale 03. 12. Cf. H. H. Wood edition of Henryson, p. xiii.

[27] In the manuscript, "Tho:" is written above the original "James," which has been crossed out by another hand. Cf. G. G. Smith, ed., *Poems of. . . Henryson,* I, ciii.

[28] Following the word "poets," the phrase "in English" is deleted in the hand of the original scribe.

Gawen Douglas made his learned & excellent translation of Virgils AEneids, who was bishop of Dunkeld, & made excellent prefaces to euery one of the twelue bookes: For this Mr Robert Henderson he was question-les a learned & a witty man, & it is pitty we haue no more of his works   being very old he dyed of a diarrhea or fluxe, of whome there goes this merry, though somewhat unsauory tale, that all phisitians hauing giuen him ouer & he lying drawing his last breath there came an old woman vnto him, who was held a witch, & asked him whether he would be cured, to whome he sayed very willingly.   then q*uo*d she there is a whikey tree ²⁹ in the lower end of yo*ur* orchard, & if you will goe and walke but thrice about it, & thrice repeate theis wordes whikey tree whikey tree take away this fluxe from me you shall be presently cured, he told her that beside he was ex-treme faint & weake it was extreme frost & snow that it was impossible for him to go: She told him that vnles he did so it was impossible he should recouer. Mr Henderson then lifting upp himselfe, & pointing to an Oken table that was in the roome, asked her & seied gude dame I pray ye tell me, if it would not do as well if I repeated thrice theis words oken burd oken burd garre me shit a hard turde.   the woman seeing herselfe derided & scorned ran out of the house in a great passion & Mr Henderson within halfe a quarter of an houre departed this life . . .³⁰

The authenticity of Kinaston's anecdote is open to doubt, for there is evidence of confusion in chronology.³¹

The poet has been persistently styled "Master Robert Henryson, schoolmaster of Dunfermline," a designation found in five instances in various late manuscripts and printed texts.³² In Henryson's day

---

²⁹ The "whikey tree" is the mountain ash, known in Scotland as the "rowan."

³⁰ Bodl. MS, Add. C. 287. Reprinted in full in G. G. Smith, ed., *Poems of . . . Henryson*, I, ciii–civ.

³¹ Kinaston says that Henryson wrote about the time of Thynne's edition of Chaucer and that "about, or a litle after," Gawin Douglas translated the *Aeneid*. This cannot be true, for the literary career of Douglas ended twenty years before the 1532 edition of Chaucer by Thynne, while on the evidence of Dunbar's *Lament*, the death of Henryson occurred sometime before 1508. Perhaps "Sr Tho: Eriskin late earle of Kelly & diuers aged schollers of the Scottish nation" told Kinaston that Douglas wrote about the time (or a little after) of Henryson, and that Henryson was the author of the sixth chapter to Chaucer's *Troilus and Criseyde* which was printed by Thynne. This would have been correct but it might have led to some confusion in the mind of Kinaston. Cf. G. G. Smith, ed., *Poems of . . . Henryson*, I, xxi, and note.

³² This designation occurs in the Charteris edition of the *Fables* in 1570; in the

the title "master" was generally conferred only upon those who had received the degree of Master of Arts. Since the poet's name does not appear on the registers of either St. Andrews or Glasgow universities, the only Scottish universities in existence at the time, Henryson may have matriculated from the University of Paris, where many of his fellow Scots studied.[33] The poet's association with Dunfermline, which was famous during this period as a royal burgh, as the site of an important Benedictine abbey, and as the residence and burial place of the Scottish kings, including Robert the Bruce, is supported by several possible allusions to the town in Henryson's poetry.[34]

Thus, in his fable *The Preiching of the Swallow*, Henryson gives a technical exposition of the preparation of flax (ll. 1825–31). Since Dunfermline was the center of spinning and linen-weaving in the poet's day (as it is today), Henryson may be describing a process which he witnessed in Dunfermline.[35] Again, in the title of a lost poem, described in the table of contents of the Asloan manuscript as "Master Robert Hendersonis dreme, On fut by forth," there may be

Harleian MS of the *Fables* of 1571; in the 1571 Bassandyne text of the *Fables;* in the 1593 Charteris edition of the *Testament;* and in the Kinaston note given in the text. *supra.* It occurs on the title page in all but the last instance. Cf. G. G. Smith, ed., *Poems of . . . Henryson*, I, xxiii ff., and H. H. Wood, *Poems and Fables of . . . Henryson*, pp. xiii ff.

[33] Cf. David Laing, ed., *The Poems and Fables of Robert Henryson*, p. xi. In fourteenth-century Scotland, the favored center of learning was Paris; in 1326, the Bishop of Moray had founded the Scots College there, and by the end of the century nine out of twenty-one supposts representing the "English nation" (British Isles, Germany, and Scandinavia) were Scots. Cf. P. H. Brown, *History of Scotland*, I, 207–8; J. H. Burton, *The Scot Abroad* (Edinburgh, 1883) Pt. II, chap. 1.

[34] Perhaps the best-known reference to Dunfermline in literature occurs in the opening lines of *Sir Patrick Spens*; Walter Scott knew the town, for in 1822, after applying to the heritors, he removed the abbey pulpit "and other relics of antiquity" to decorate the entrance hall of Abbotsford. Cf. J. C. R. Buckner, *Clark's Guide to Dunfermline*, p. 9. The town is known in America as the birthplace of Andrew Carnegie; it is situated about fifteen miles north of Edinburgh, across the Firth of Forth.

[35] The first record of the weaving industry in Dunfermline occurs in 1491, when six "wabsters" were charged with "strubblance" (breach of the peace). Cf. G. G. Smith, ed., *Poems of . . . Henryson*, I, 28.

an allusion to the countryside south of Dunfermline.[36] Further, the opening lines of the poet's *Abbay Walk* mention an abbey "fair to se," which may refer to the Benedictine foundation.[37] In the poem, *Sum Practysis of Medecyne,* the expression "fra lawdian to lundin" occurs, which would come naturally to a person living in Dunfermline.[38] And finally, the mention in the *Testament* of a gate, a village half a mile away, and a spital-house (ll. 388–91), bears a close resemblance to landmarks in modern Dunfermline.[39]

Although Henryson's choice and treatment of subject matter support the designation of schoolmaster, there is no proof that the poet was one. It is probable, however, that a grammar school, located within the precincts of the abbey, existed in Henryson's day,[40] and although this school was under the jurisdiction of the abbots, its schoolmasters need not have been monks.[41] This may throw some light upon the fact that the poet is nowhere designated by the ecclesiastical title "clericus" or "presbyter." Moreover, three deeds in the Chartulary of Dunfermline, in the years 1477–78, are witnessed by "Magister Robertus Henrison notarius publicus." [42]

In the records of the University of Glasgow, the following entry occurs:

Anno Domini etc. [M.CCCC] lxij° die decimo mensis Septembris Incorporatus fuit venerabilis vir Magister Robertus Henrisone in Artibus Licentiatus et in Decretis Bachalarius.[43]

---

[36] *Ibid.,* I, lxxviii.

[37] Cf. David Laing, ed., *Poems and Fables of. . . Henryson,* p. xix.

[38] Literally: from Lothian to Lundin (now Lundin Links, Fifeshire), i.e., from South to North. Cf. G. G. Smith, ed., *Poems of . . . Henryson,* I, xxiv–xxv.

[39] It has been suggested that the gate refers to an historic gate in the south wall of the monastery on Priory Lane, that the village alludes to the outlying settlement of Nethertown, and that the spital-house designates St. Leonard's hospital. Cf. E. Henderson, ed., *The Annals of Dunfermline,* pp. 169–70. In the poet's day, the hospital may have been used for lepers.

[40] Cf. David Laing, ed., *Poems and Fables of . . . Henryson,* pp. lv–lvii.

[41] Cf. G. Chalmers, ed., *Robene and Makyne, and the Testament of Cresseid,* p. vii, note 2.

[42] Cf. David Laing, ed., *Poems and Fables of . . . Henryson,* p. xiii.

[43] *Ibid.,* pp. xxxvii–xl.

David Laing, who made an exhaustive search for biographical material throughout Scotland, suggests that Henryson became a fellow for
the purpose of reading lectures in law, a suggestion that is supported
by the poet's frequent and accurate use of legal terms.[44]

With the exception of two personal allusions—in the *Testament,*
the poet speaks of himself as a man of age (l. 29) and in the *Orpheus
and Eurydice,* he says he cannot sing a note (l. 242)—these are the
recorded facts and conjectures concerning Henryson's life. In view
of the scantiness of the material, the student of Henryson is forced
back to a study of the internal evidence in the poet's verse. Very little
has been accomplished in this direction, but, since most of the texts
are now well established, the time is ripe for such work.

[44] Cf. *infra*, pp. 28–32.

Chapter II

POLITICS, RELIGION, AND LAW

*A*LTHOUGH THE FIFTEENTH CENTURY in Scotland was a golden age of Scottish culture, it was also an age of transition, of political turmoil and civil war, of unscrupulous violence and bloody treachery. The Stewart monarchs dominated the period in unbroken sequence, but all four of them struggled to maintain themselves against treachery and all four met with violent deaths.

The Scottish Wars of Independence (1286–1371) had paralleled roughly the Hundred Years' War in England, and despite internal dissension, England's invading armies had been turned back. While the war with England had produced genuine national unity and had helped to blend Celtic and Anglo-Norman elements in Scottish civilization, the battle of Harlaw (1411) had shown that clan and regional animosities were easily revived; and in fact they remained a threat throughout the century.

James I, who reigned from 1424 to 1437, an energetic and head-strong king noted for his reforms, instituted strong measures against the rebellious nobles, but these measures failed to prevent his murder by his fellow-countryman, Sir Robert Graham, at Perth. His successor, James II, who ruled from 1437 to 1460, was barely able to keep his head above the treacherous tides of insurrection. He held the power-ful house of Douglas in check only by murdering the eighth Earl and by defeating the ninth Earl on the battlefield in 1455. Having maintained the Stewart line in times more unsettled than those of his father, James II met death by the accidental bursting of a cannon at the siege of Roxburgh.

The reign of James III (1460–88) is of particular interest because Robert Henryson presumably flourished during this period. James III, the weakest of the Stewarts, came to the throne at a time when his kingdom was split over the question of loyalty to England. The queen mother, Mary of Gueldres, aided by John, Earl of Ross and Lord of the Isles, and the exiled Earl of Douglas, favored the Yorkists and aided Edward IV of England. Bishop Kennedy, one of Scotland's greatest churchmen, and the majority of the nobles followed James II's policy of helping Henry VI and the Lancastrians. James III procrastinated while feuds flickered throughout the land. Religious abuses were sanctioned by church and crown, and legal reforms remained the dream of a few enlightened men. Kidnapped twice during his reign, James III was finally murdered by his own nobles, who had enlisted the support of his son, the future James IV.

In the reign of James IV (1488–1513), although rebellion continued, comparative order was established and Scotland reached a peak of prosperity. This prosperity was checked by the disastrous battle of Flodden (1513), and Scotland returned to the semibarbarism of former days, from which it did not emerge for nearly a century.

It is noteworthy that Henryson, living in these turbulent times of bloodshed and corruption, did not retreat entirely into the artificial world of the dream-allegory, as did many of his contemporaries. On the contrary, the poet refers frequently and sometimes with considerable warmth to the events of the day. Some of these references are couched in veiled terms for obvious reasons, and most of them occur in the *Morall Fabillis of Esope*.

I

The concluding *moralitas* to Henryson's fable of the *Lion and the Mouse* contains vigorous criticism which, if it had been asserted independently, might well have goaded a harassed monarch into hasty vengeance. The poet says (ll. 1573–79, 1587–93, 1608–19):

As I suppois, this mychtie gay Lyoun
May signifie ane Prince, or Empriour,
Ane Potestate, or yit ane King with Croun,
Quhilk suld be walkrife gyde and Governour
Of his pepill, that takis na labour
To reule and steir the land, and Justice keip,
Bot lyis still in lustis, sleuth, and sleip

.   .   .   .   .

Thir lytill Myis ar bot the commountie,
Wantoun, unwyse, without correctioun:
Thair Lordis and Princis quhen that thay se
Of Justice mak nane executioun,
Thay dreid na thing to mak Rebellioun,
And disobey, for quhy thay stand nane aw,
That garris thame thair Soveranis misknaw.

.   .   .   .   .

Thir rurall men, that stentit hes the Net,
In quhilk the Lyoun suddandlie wes tane,
Waittit alway amendis for to get
(For hurt men wrytis in the Marbill Stane).
Mair till expound as now I lett allane,
Bot King and Lord may weill wit quhat I mene:
Figure heirof oftymis hes bene sene.

Quhen this wes said (quod Esope): "my fair child,
I the beseik and all men for to pray
That tressoun of this cuntrie be exyld,
And Justice Regne, and Lordis keip thair fay
Unto thair Soverane King, baith nycht and day." [1]

The fable to which Henryson affixes these lines is the familiar story of the Lion caught in the net. The Lion, says the poet, may signify a king with crown who makes no effort to rule and influence the land but lies still in lusts, sloth, and sleep. These characteristics fit the contemporary view of James III, for this monarch, unlike the

---

[1] H. H. Wood, ed., *The Poems and Fables of Robert Henryson*, pp. 56–57. Quotations from Henryson's works are taken from this edition.

Stewarts who preceded and followed him, was regarded as a weak dilettante with a notable lack of interest in the welfare of his country.[2]

An apt historical analogy for the capture of the Lion may be found in the reign of James III; in 1466, a group of powerful nobles led by Sir Alexander Boyd kidnapped the king and imprisoned him at Edinburgh.[3] James III was eventually released and Sir Alexander pardoned.[4] Since the Lion is freed from the net, his experience suggests a temporary imprisonment such as the king endured. Henryson is emphatic on the subject of treason, exhorting the lords to keep faith with their king, and it may be added that treason among the nobles was particularly frequent during the reign of James III.[5] The poet's mysterious statement that he will not explain any more at this time, but the king and lords may well know what he means since examples have frequently been seen hereabouts (ll. 1612–14), reinforces the impression that Henryson is alluding to actual contemporary events.[6] And finally, it should be noted that in this fable alone

[2] Cf. P. H. Brown, *History of Scotland*, I, 288; S. Cowan, *The Royal House of Stuart*, I, 257.

[3] Although both James II and James IV were kidnapped during their minorities, only James III was captured and imprisoned during his reign.

[4] Boyd's motive seems to have been a lust for power. The king accomplished the downfall of the Boyds during the absence of the family leaders as envoys to Norway in 1469. Cf. P. H. Brown, *History of Scotland*, I, 261–62.

[5] James I put down two rebellions, one led by Albany and the other by the Lord of the Isles; James II finally overcame the Douglases in the persons of the eighth and ninth earls; James III, however, warred continuously with the Boyds, the Lord of the Isles, the Duke of Albany, and was murdered by his own nobles in 1488. The reign of James IV was relatively free from rebellion. Cf. P. H. Brown, *History of Scotland*, I, 211 ff.

[6] It may be that the poet is afraid to be more explicit concerning a well-known crime. In the lines immediately preceding his refusal to reveal anything further, Henryson says that these rural men, who have spread the net in which the Lion was suddenly taken, always hunt for amends (a reference to the numerous feuds of the time?), for hurt men write in the marble stone (ll. 1608–11). Can this last phrase be the colloquial equivalent of "Dead men tell no tales," i.e., once buried, all that is left is a man's name on a marble gravestone? The murder of James III suggests itself, for James IV was implicated in the murder of his father, and the subject must have been a dangerous one. Cf. P. H. Brown, *History of Scotland*, I, 285–87. On the other

Henryson goes to extravagant lengths to keep himself in the background: not only is the vehicle for this criticism a dream-vision
from which the poet wakes at the conclusion of the *moralitas*, but
also the criticism itself is placed in the mouth of Aesop. In view of
the despotic power of the feudal lords, Henryson's precautions may
have been quite necessary.

   To his fable, *The Taill of the Sōe & Air of the forsaid Foxe, callit
Father wer: Alswa the Parliemĕt of four-futtit Beistis, haldin be the
Lyoun,* Henryson prefixes the following account of filial ingratitude
which has little relevance to the fable itself (ll. 796–837):

> This foirsaid ffoxe, that deit ffor his misdeid,
> Had not ane barne wes gottin richteouslie,
> Till airschip be Law that micht succeid,
> Except ane Sone, quhilk in Adulterie
> He gotten had in purches privelie,
> And till his Name wes callit Father war,
> That luifit weill with pultrie to tig and tar.

> It followis weill be ressoun naturall,
> And gre be gre, off richt comparisoun,
> Off euill cummis war, off war cummis werst of all,
> Off wrangus geir cummis fals successioun.
> This ffoxe, Bastard of generatioun,
> Off verray kinde behuifit to be fals;
> Swa wes his Father, and his Grandschir als.

> As Nature will, seikand his meit be sent,
> Off cace he fand his ffatheris Carioun,
> Nakit, new slane; and till him hes he went,
> Tuke up his heid, and on his kne fell doun,
> Thankand grit God off that conclusioun;
> And said, "Now sall I bruke, sen I am air,
> The boundis quhair thow wes wont ffor to repair."

> "Fy! Covetice, unkynd, and venemous:
> The Sone wes fane he fand his ffather deid,

---

hand, the phrase "hurt men write in the marble stone" may mean: an injured man
is slow to forgive an injury. Such sentiments would well fit the times.

Be suddand schot, ffor deidis odious,
That he micht ringe, and raxe in till his steid,
Dreidand na thing the samin lyfe to leid,
In thift, and reif, as did his ffather befoir;
Bot to the end attent he tuke no moir.

Yit nevertheles, throw Naturall pietie,
The Carioun upon his bak he tais.
"Now find I weill this prouerb trew" (quod he),
" 'Ay rinnis the ffoxe, als lang as he fute hais.' "
Syne with the Corps unto ane peitpoit gais,
Off watter ffull, and kest him in the deip,
And to the Devill he gaif his banis to keip.

O fulische man! plungit in warldynes,
To conqueis warldlie gude, and gold, and rent,
To put thy Saull in pane, or hevines,
To richt thy air, quhilk efter thow art went,
Have he thy gude, he takis bot small tent
To execute, to do, to satisfie
Thy letter will, thy det, and legacie.[7]

This passage contains many details which appear to refer to some specific person. The poet says that "Father War" (worse than his. father) was begotten in adultery and that there was no legitimate son and rightful heir; this Fox, a bastard by birth, is naturally like his father and grandfather before him; moreover, the Fox is pleased by his father's death, for he thanks God and says that now that he is heir he will enjoy the bounds to which his father used to repair.

The history of the successive Lords of the Isles forms an interesting parallel. The Lords of the Isles were a constant threat to the Stewart line for at least three generations, from Alexander, third Lord of the Isles, who was a thorn in the side of James I, to Donald Dhu, who was finally subdued by James IV in 1507.[8] Henryson's remarks point

---

[7] H. H. Wood, ed., *Poems and Fables of . . . Henryson*, pp. 30–31.
[8] Cf. P. H. Brown, *History of Scotland*, I, 213–14, 251 ff.

to Angus, for Angus was not only of the third generation but also of illegitimate birth.[9] Further, Angus led the discontented followers of his own father, John, fourth Lord of the Isles, against their chief and defeated him in a decisive naval battle near Tobermory.[10] The Fox's statement that now that he is heir he will enjoy the bounds to which his father used to repair furthers the parallel, for the motive which had led Angus to revolt against his father was a resentment of the fact that John had subjected himself to James III.[11] Thus, having defeated his father, Angus was free to violate the boundary treaties between John and the king. The rebellion of Angus against his father is an exception to the code of clan loyalty for which the age is noted, and makes it difficult to find any other historical analogy for Henryson's allusions.

At the end of his fable, *The Taill of the Wolf and the Wedder,* which tells how the Wether, after the death of the Dog, wears the Dog's skin and chases the Wolf until the trick is discovered and its wearer slain, Henryson adds the following remarks concerning base-born upstarts (ll. 2595–2615):

> Heir may thow se that riches of array
> Will cause pure men presumpteous for to be;
> They think thay hald of nane, be they als gay,
> Bot counterfute ane Lord in all degre.
> Out of thair cais in pryde thay clym sa hie,
> That thay forbeir thair better in na steid,
> Quhill sum man tit thair heillis over thair heid.
>
> Richt swa in service uther sum exceidis,
> And thay haif withgang, welth, and cherising,
> That thay will lychtlie Lordis in thair deidis,

---

[9] *Idem.*   [10] *Ibid.,* I, 251 ff. Angus died in 1490.

[11] Although subdued by James III in 1476, John had been a dangerous subject for many years. In 1462, he had made a secret treaty with Edward IV of England, whereby John was to dominate Scotland north of the Forth after the next English invasion which he was supposed to assist. Armed with this treaty, John had confiscated crown rents and customs and maintained a series of ruthless feuds against the king's allies. Cf. P. H. Brown, *History of Scotland,* I, 267–68; S. Cowan, *op. cit.,* I, 242 ff.

And lukis not to thair blude, nor thair offspring:
Bot yit nane wait how lang that reull will ring;
Bot he was wyse, that bad his Sone considder:
Bewar in welth, for Hall benkis ar rycht slidder.

Thairfoir I counsell men of everilk stait
To knaw thame self, and quhome thay suld forbeir,
And fall not with thair better in debait;
Suppois thay be als galland in thair geir,
It settis na servand for to uphald weir,
Nor clym so hie, quhill he fall of the ledder;
Bot think upon the Wolf, and on the wedder.[12]

The poet criticizes poor men who become presumptuous because of
their finery, who think they are subject to no one, and who counterfeit
a lord in every way. These men have liberty, wealth, and favor; they
disparage the deeds of the lords; and they do not look to their blood
or descent. Men of every state should know whom not to molest and
should not argue with their betters. No matter how well outfitted
a servant may be, he should not carry on a feud.

James III was particularly unfortunate in that he continually an-
tagonized his own nobles, not only by his lack of interest in the welfare of the state, but also by his obvious preference for the company
of certain favorites to whom he gave great power. These favorites
were not warriors and members of the nobility, but commoners who
practiced peaceful arts; among them were the musician, William
Roger; the tailor, James Hommyle; and the architect, Thomas Cochrane. The most thoroughly hated and despised was Cochrane, whose
ascendency over James III has been referred to as the main cause of
the many disasters which beset the reign.[13]

On the other hand, the nobles openly admired James III's two
younger brothers, Alexander, Duke of Albany, and John, Earl of
Mar, who were typical Scottish chiefs of aggressive disposition and

[12] H. H. Wood, *Poems and Fables of . . . Henryson*, p. 89.
[13] P. H. Brown, *History of Scotland*, I, 269; S. Cowan, *op. cit.*, I, 261.

great physical prowess.[14] In 1479, James threw them both into jail where the Earl of Mar died, and popular opinion fastened the blame upon Cochrane, who promptly obtained the lands and title of the dead prince. The Duke of Albany escaped, however, and with the aid of Edward IV assembled an army and marched north in 1482. James III, on his way to repel the invaders with his favorites at his elbow, was overtaken by another and stronger army of his own nobles, who demanded the custody of the favorites. Upon the king's refusal, the nobles imprisoned him at Edinburgh, put his favorites to death, and made a separate truce with the invading Albany.[15]

Henryson's criticism of baseborn upstarts fits the favorites of James III closely. In fact, the poet's reference to servants and those who are in favor ("cherising") makes it difficult to consider any other group. In particular, Cochrane was baseborn, although he attained "withgang, welth, and cherising," and he was noted for his "riches of array" [16] which, combined with his new title of Earl of Mar, indicate that he truly "counterfute ane Lord in all degre." It is clear, moreover, that Cochrane did not allow questions of "blude" or "off-spring" to deter him, that he acted as if he "hald of none," and that he "will lychtlie Lordis in thair deidis" and engaged his "better in debait." That Cochrane molested those whom he should not and "uphald weir" against the nobles in the persons of the king's brothers is a matter of record.[17]

In his *Taill of the Paddock & the Mous,* Henryson narrates the story of the Frog who treacherously attempts to drown a Mouse, but who is captured and eaten by a Kite. The poet adds the following moral directed against deceitful companions (ll. 2910–33):

[14] *Ibid.,* I, 257.

[15] Cf. P. H. Brown, *History of Scotland,* I, 276–78; A. M. Mackenzie, *The Rise of the Stewarts,* pp. 280–81.

[16] Cf. Æ. J. G. Mackay, ed., *The Historie and Cronicles of Scotland . . . by Robert Lindesay of Pitscottie,* I, 174.

[17] Cf. J. Taylor, *Pictorial History of Scotland,* I, 355 and note.

My Brother, gif thow will tak advertence
Be this Fabill, thow may persave and se,
It passis far all kynd of Pestilence,
Ane wickit mynd with wordis fair and sle.
Be war thairfore, with quhome thow fallowis the;
To the wer better beir the stane barrow,
For all thy dayis to delf quhill thow may dre,
Than to be machit with ane wickit marrow.

Ane fals Intent under any fair pretence
Hes causit mony Innocent for to de.
Grit folie is to gif over sone credence
To all that speikis fairlie unto the.
Ane silkin toung, ane hart of crueltie,
Smytis more sore than ony schot of arrow.
Brother, gif thow be wyse, I reid the fle,
To matche the with any thrawart, fenyeit marrow.

I warne the als, it is grit nekligence
To bind the fast quhair thow wes frank and fre;
Fra thow be bund, thow may mak na defence
To saif thy lyfe, nor yit thy libertie.
This simpill counsall, brother, tak of me,
And it to cun perqueir se thow not tarrow,
Better but stryfe to leif allane in le
Than to be matchit with ane wickit marrow.[18]

Henryson is warning his reader to beware of wicked minds with fair and sly words, false intentions under fair pretense, and a silken tongue with a cruel heart. It is great folly to give credence to all who speak fair, great negligence to bind yourself fast where you were free. Once you are bound, you cannot defend your life and liberty. Therefore, the poet repeats ominously, beware of your companions, for any other evil is preferable to that of a crooked, deceitful companion ("thrawart, fenyeit marrow").

The poet is insisting upon the kind of treachery accomplished by

[18] H. H. Wood, ed., *Poems and Fables of . . . Henryson*, pp. 100–101.

a close friend with deceptive manners and appearance. The outstanding example of such treachery in the reign of James III may be found in the person of Alexander, Duke of Albany and younger brother of the king. Arriving with his English army after the Scottish nobles had already imprisoned James and put his favorites to death, Albany made a truce with the nobles and then unexpectedly rescued the king. For a brief interval, the brothers appeared to be wholly reconciled. James forgave Albany, and it is said that they shared the same chamber, table, and bed.[19] But Albany, having been rewarded by an appointment to the Lieutenant Generalship of the Realm, filled important positions with his own supporters and reopened his treasonable plot with Edward IV of England.[20] James retaliated at the last moment by depriving Albany's friends of their offices. Rendered helpless, Albany confessed and swore allegiance anew, whereupon James forgave his brother once more. This state of affairs lasted but a short time, for Albany immediately resumed his intrigues. His ambitions were finally crushed by the death of his powerful ally, Edward IV, in 1483.[21]

In the case of James III and Albany, Henryson's warning that when "thow be bund, thow may mak na defence to saif thy lyfe, nor yit thy libertie" would apply literally. Albany, known as the father of chivalry in France because of his pleasing manners and speech,[22] was famous for his ability to "speikis fairlie," for his "silkin toung," and for his "wordis fair." Further, there is no doubt of the "fals Intent under ane fair pretence" toward his vacillating brother, the king. The poet says that it is great negligence "to bind the fast quhair thow wes frank and fre," which is precisely what James did, not once but over and over again. To the king, Albany was surely a "thrawart, fenyeit

---

[19] Cf. J. Taylor, *op. cit.,* I, 357.

[20] The plot was well known, and there was considerable opposition among the nobles and the gentry long before James acted. Cf. P. H. Brown, *History of Scotland,* I, 279 ff., and A. M. Mackenzie, *The Rise of the Stewarts,* pp. 284 ff.

[21] P. H. Brown, *History of Scotland,* I, 281 ff.; S. Cowan, *op. cit.,* I, 265.

[22] Cf. P. H. Brown, *History of Scotland,* I, 270.

marrow," and the situation must have been particularly distressing to those who were loyal to James III. Finally, there máy be a hidden reference to fraternal relationships in the poet's use of the word "brother" in addressing the reader.[23]

The possibility that the foregoing passages in Henryson's verse may refer to political events in the reign of James III is supported by the known facts of the poet's life. Further, if the suggested historical analogies are convincing, we may deduce a tentative date for the composition of the *Fables*. The possible allusion to the kidnapping of James III in 1466 would set an anterior date to the *Fables,* while the suggested reference to Angus, who was notorious for his lawless escapades from 1480 to 1490, when he was assassinated, would tend to narrow the period in which the *Fables* were composed. Since Cochrane was hanged in 1482 and Albany was rendered powerless by the death of Edward IV in 1483, we may arrive at a posterior date, at which time these issues were of no further interest. Thus, the *Fables* were perhaps written in the late seventies or the early eighties.

In the process of discussing the possibility of specific parallels, however, we meet with certain indisputable facts concerning the poet's times. He comments upon negligent monarchs and the crime of treason; he mentions the untrustworthiness of the nobles, the presumptuousness of baseborn upstarts, and the sin of filial ingratitude no matter how deserved it may be. That there was adequate cause for these observations in the poet's day is abundantly clear, and they form a penetrating commentary on the age.

II

Robert Henryson's comments on religious matters are highly revealing. The church reached its greatest material development in

[23] For some reason, Henryson suddenly slips into the habit of addressing the reader in this manner (cf. ll. 2910, 2924, 2930). In other fables, the poet uses such phrases as "friends," "worthy folk," "ye lords," "readers," and "men of every station." In each case, the appellation is chosen to fit the context. The use of "brother" suggests that Henryson was pointing his reference to James III and Albany.

Scotland at the close of the thirteenth century. By the fifteenth century, because of the intervention of the crown and the shortsighted ecclesiastical policy of sanctioning that intervention, the church was well on the road which was to end in the Reformation of 1560. The rapid deterioration in the morals of both the clergy and the government of the church was underway in the reign of James III,[24] and what is generally considered the turning point in Scottish church history took place at the abbey where Henryson presumably lived. In 1472, James III broke all precedent by appointing Henry Creichton to the position of Abbot of Dunfermline over the heads of the monks who had duly elected Alexander Thomson, and the appointment was confirmed by a papal bull.[25]

In his *Orpheus and Eurydice,* Henryson describes the wanderings of Orpheus in hell (ll. 338–44):

> Thair saw he mony paip and cardynall,
> In haly kirk quhilk did abusioun,
> and bischopis in thair pontificall,
> Be symonie and wrang Intrusioun;
> abbottis and all men of religioun,
> ffor evill disponyng of thair place and rent,
> In flame of fyre wer bittirly torment.

Although the poet is ostensibly relating an old story, it may well have taken courage not only to name such serious crimes in this Dantesque list of high churchmen,[26] but also to specify "abbottis" and the crime of "wrang Intrusioun"—a reasonably accurate description of the method by which James III established his own appointee at Dunfermline. There is no doubt that such abuses existed in Henryson's

---

[24] Cf. P. H. Brown, *History of Scotland,* I, 263.

[25] Comments on the significance of the event are summarized by I. F. Grant, *The Social and Economic Development of Scotland before 1603,* pp. 220–21. Cf. E. Henderson, ed., *Annals of Dunfermline,* pp. 162–63.

[26] Cf. *Inferno,* xix. As to the seriousness of the sin of simony, cf. W. Murison, *Sir David Lyndsay,* pp. 102–5, 157. Cf. further A. I. Cameron, *The Apostolic Camera and Scottish Benefices,* pp. xxxi ff.

day,[27] but to comment unfavorably and specifically upon them may not have been too safe a matter.[28]

In his fable of *The Fox and the Wolf,* Henryson illustrates the abuses to which the act of confession may be put. The Fox, believing that his time has come, seeks out Friar Wolf "Waitskaith" (one-who-waits-to-do-injury), who is described as follows (ll. 666–69):

> Ane worthie Doctour in Divinitie,
> Freir Wolff Waitskaith, in science wonder sle,
> To preich and pray wes new cummit ffra the Closter
> With Beidis in hand, sayand his pater noster.

The Fox's address to his "Gostlie ffather under God" is double-edged satire (ll. 667–83):

> "Ye ar Mirrour, Lanterne, and sicker way,
> Suld gyde sic sempill folk as me to grace.
> Your bair feit, and your Russet Coull off gray,
> Your lene cheik, your paill pietious face,
> Schawis to me your perfite halines.
> For weill wer him, that anis in his lyve
> Had hap to yow his sinnis ffor to schryve."

The Wolf's bare feet and gray cowl would indeed have been considered unpretentious in Henryson's day.[29] After the Fox has confessed the sins of theft and robbery, the Wolf proceeds with the three questions included in the Catholic sacrament of penance: *contritio, confessio,* and *satisfactio* (ll. 698–99):[30]

> "Art thow contrite, and sorie in thy Spreit
> For thy trespas?"

---

[27] Cf. G. G. Coulton, *Scottish Abbeys and Social Life,* pp. 253 ff.; J. Dowden, *The Medieval Church in Scotland,* p. 127.

[28] A century later, when criticism of the church became more prevalent, Lyndsay still hesitated to bring charges against the clergy. Cf. W. Murison, *op. cit.,* p. 58.

[29] Cf. J. Dowden, *op. cit.,* p. 248; I. F. Grant, *Social and Economic Development,* p. 322.

[30] Cf. G. G. Smith, ed., *The Poems of Robert Henryson,* I, 13–14. The general practice regarding penance is described by J. Dowden, *op. cit.,* p. 244.

The Fox replies that he is not contrite, and the Wolf continues (ll. 705–6):

> "Sen thow can not forthink thy wickitnes,
> Will thow forbeir in tyme to cum and mend?"

The Fox refuses but the Wolf continues undisturbed (ll. 712–15):

> "Weill" (quod the Wolff) "thow wantis pointis twa,
> Belangand to perfyte Confessioun.
> To the thrid part off penitence let us ga:
> Will thow tak pane for thy transgressioun?"

The Fox reluctantly agrees to a little penance, "swa it wer licht, Schort, and not grevand to my tendernes," and is granted full remission. He is to eat no meat until Easter, but twice a week he may taste "puddingis" (forced meat), blood, and the heads, feet, and paunches (of fowl or sheep).[31] However, he soon breaks even this light penance.

It is difficult to determine how dangerous a course Henryson was following, but it is certain that since the Scottish Reformation, in contrast to that of England, was considerably delayed, the poet was running counter to the explicit attitude of both church and state, and it is possible that he was incurring a greater risk than may at first be realized.[32] I have been unable to find in Scottish literature an earlier or more extensive illustration of the ineffectiveness of the act of confession.[33]

III

It is clear that Henryson had a detailed knowledge of law. The subject was not simple, for Scotland, unlike England, had no body

---

[31] The poet does not report the *confessio,* saying that it would not be fitting to do so. Cf. ll. 694–96.

[32] Cf. I. F. Grant, *Social and Economic Development,* pp. 226–27.

[33] The famous criticisms of the church found in the poems of Dunbar and Lyndsay (cf. *Kitteis Confessioun*) were made well after Henryson's day.

of common law to guide its decisions and there were continual but ineffective attempts to make a digest of the laws in order to remedy the confusion.[34] Two systems of courts existed side by side in open competition: the civil and the ecclesiastical. The civil courts consisted primarily of the itinerant Justice-Ayres presided over by sheriffs who sat at the Assizes.[35] In Henryson's day, these sheriffs were powerful men who lived in royal castles, administered the crown estates, collected fines, and tried cases.[36] The ecclesiastical courts, however, were better established and organized; they monopolized a large percentage of civil cases as well as the usual consistorial business; their judges were reputed to be the most learned men in the land; [37] and although they were notorious for their venality, they were extending their powers rapidly at this time.[38]

In his fable, *The Sheep and the Dog,* Henryson criticizes adversely both the civil and the ecclesiastical courts. The fable proper tells the story of the Dog who hales a Sheep into the church court to recover a piece of bread. The judge, a fraudulent Wolf who has "Authoritie and Jurisdictioun," issues a "Citatioun" (ll. 1155-59):

> I, Maister Wolff, partles off fraud and gyle,
> Under the panis off hie Suspensioun,
> Off grit Cursing, and Interdictioun,
> Schir Scheip, I charge the for to compeir,
> And answer to ane Doig befoir me heir.

The ecclesiastical penalties, *suspensio totalis, excommunicatio major,* and *interdictio,* which the Wolf lists, were the customary weapons of the church courts.[39] The frequent use of these penalties, however,

---

[34] Cf. J. Taylor, *op. cit.,* I, 367 ff.

[35] The burgh courts, which nominally dealt with all cases within the burghs except the four pleas of the crown, were also civil courts, but in practice they were far less important. Cf. I. F. Grant, *Social and Economic Development,* p. 138.

[36] *Ibid.,* pp. 28–31.

[37] Cf. C. Innes, *Sketches of Early Scotch History and Social Progress,* p. 263.

[38] Cf. W. Murison, *op. cit.,* pp. 109–10.

[39] Cf. G. G. Smith, ed., *Poems of . . . Henryson,* I, 20–21.

even to enforce payment of small debts, shows that they must have become increasingly ineffective.[40]

A Raven is made "Apparitour," an officer of a church court, and he serves the summons and endorses the writ. The trial starts at sundown, with the Fox as clerk and notary, and the Kite and Vulture as advocates at the bar. The Sheep, although abject with fear, reveals a knowledge of the law, for he queries the jurisdiction of the court, declining the judge, the time, and the place (l. 1187). Since the trial is being held at night, an unlawful hour, the Sheep is technically correct.[41]

Temporarily foiled, the Wolf bids the parties choose two arbiters according to law, and the Bear and the Badger are selected (ll. 1212–22) :

> And thairupon, as Jugis, thay sat doun,
> And held ane lang quhyle disputatioun,
> Seikand full mony Decreitis off the Law,
> And Glosis als, the veritie to knaw.
>
> Of Civile Law volumnis full mony thay revolve,
> The Codies and Digestis new and ald;
> Contrait, Prostrait Argumentis thay resolve,
> Sum objecting, and sum can hald;
> For prayer, or price, trow ye that thay wald fald?
> Bot hald the glose, and Text of the Decreis,
> As trew Jugis; I beschrew thame ay that leis.

This satire on the various authorities consulted by the two arbiters reflects the state of confusion in which the law existed in Henryson's day. The reference to the "Codies and Digestis" may be an allusion to the ridiculous division of the Pandects by Bulgarius in the twelfth century.[42]

The two arbiters decide that the court has jurisdiction, and Henry-

---

[40] Cf. G. G. Coulton, *Scottish Abbeys*, p. 59; W. Murison, *op. cit.*, p. 145.
[41] Cf. G. G. Smith, ed., *Poems of . . . Henryson*, I, 20–21.
[42] Cf. Lord Hailes, *Ancient Scottish Poems*, p. 329.

son states accurately that the Sheep has no appeal from a decision by arbiters of his own choosing.[43] Thus the trial concludes (ll. 1245–47):

> The Wolff chargit the Scheip, without delay,
> Under the panis off Interdictioun,
> The soume off silver, or the breid, to pay.

The Sheep is left naked and bare in the field.

In the fable proper, Henryson shows his detailed knowledge of ecclesiastical law by emphasizing the absurdities in the *form of process* of the church courts; in the *moralitas* to the same fable, the poet turns to the civil courts.[44] The Sheep becomes the poor commons and the Wolf a sheriff (ll. 1265–68):

> This Wolf I likkin to ane Schiref stout,
> Quhilk byis ane forfalt at the Kingis hand,
> And hes with him ane cursit Assyis about,
> And dytis all the pure men up on land.

This sheriff, who buys fines from the king and indicts poor men, is the judge of the civil courts who presides over the Assizes of the itinerant Justice-Ayres. Henryson had valid grounds for criticism, since the Justice-Ayres were notoriously corrupt and there are frequent references in the statute books to judges who neglected to uphold the laws.[45]

The Raven is likened to a coroner (ll. 1272–78):

> This Ravin I likkin to ane fals Crownair,
> Quhilk hes ane portioun of the Inditement,
> And passis furth befoir the Justice Air,
> All misdoaris to bring to Jugement;

---

[43] Cf. G. G. Smith, ed., *Poems of . . . Henryson,* I, 22.

[44] Cf. Hailes, *op. cit.,* p. 328. Lord Hailes inferred that since the satire of the fable proper is aimed at the church and that of the *moralitas* at the civil courts, the poet "stood more in awe of the court spiritual than of the temporal." *Ibid.,* p. 329. This inference seems unjustified. The action would have obtained at law in either court, and Henryson appears to be taking the opportunity to criticize both.

[45] Cf. J. Taylor, *op. cit.,* I, 367.

> Bot luke, gif he wes of ane trew Intent,
> To scraip out Johne, and wryte in Will, or Wat,
> And tak ane bud at boith the parteis tat.

This coroner is an officer of the civil court, and his "portioun," which he alters for bribes, is the list of offenders furnished by the local authorities.[46] Thus, all of the court officers have their civil counterparts who are similarly corrupt.

In the Sheep's lament, affixed to the end of the fable, Henryson comments vigorously on the state of the law in his time (ll. 1300–1306):

> Se how this cursit sone of covetice,
> Loist hes baith lawtie and eik Law.
> Now few or nane will execute Justice,
> In falt of quhome the pure man is overthraw.
> The veritie, suppois the Juge it knaw,
> He is so blindit with affectioun,
> But dreid, for micht, he lettis the richt go doun.

Covetousness has destroyed both loyalty and law; at this time, few or none will execute justice, for the lack of which the poor man is overthrown; although the judge knows the truth, he is so blinded by partiality without doubt that, because of force, he lets the right go down. Thus, this indictment of the legal process seems to apply to civil and ecclesiastical courts alike, and there is little doubt of Henryson's thorough knowledge and accurate description of both.[47]

By uniting Henryson's allusions to the subjects of politics, religion, and law, we arrive at a revealing portrait of the age. The poet's interest in the fundamental problems of his day was exceeded only by his outspoken attitude toward them. In each case, his point of view is characterized by detailed knowledge and keen understanding, which sheds new light upon the history of the times.

[46] Cf. G. G. Smith, ed., *Poems of . . . Henryson,* I, 22.

[47] In his tendency to blame "covetice" for the loss of loyalty and law, Henryson is following the standard teaching of the church in opposing usury. Cf. R. H. Tawney, *Religion and the Rise of Capitalism,* pp. 106 *et passim.*

Chapter III

THE SOCIO-ECONOMIC
BACKGROUND

*F*EUDALISM developed more slowly in Scotland than in England, and lingered on much later, yet the ties of Scottish feudalism were never as strict or well defined. Feudal relationships, particularly in the highlands, existed side by side with clan or tribal customs, and the concept of "loyalty," for example, was important to both, although for different and sometimes conflicting reasons. Unlike England, Scotland produced no class of yeomen to cushion the transition from a feudal to a mercantile economy. Thus, the general growth and decline of feudalism in Scotland appears to have been more confused and less clearly marked than in England.

In Henryson's Scotland perhaps the greatest single socio-economic fact was instability. In addition to devastating plagues, two circumstances helped make stability impossible: first, the feudal lords were constantly on the verge of overpowering the crown and sweeping away whatever advances had been made toward a centralized government; secondly, large tracts of land, the all-important source of manpower as well as revenue, were constantly changing hands either by reversion or by the innumerable chances of war. In the course of his writing, Henryson has occasion to refer to several phases of this socio-economic scene. These references may be conveniently brought together in the present chapter. The poet presents a detailed picture, for example, of the social and economic differences between various groups in his day. The contrast between living conditions in town and country in fifteenth-century Scotland was great. The country

Scots, living in widely scattered groups of primitive huts, supported themselves by agriculture which was carried on at a subsistence level; the town Scots, living in substantial stone houses, carried on foreign trade under the protection of special privileges.[1]

In his fable, *The Taill of the Uponlandis Mous, and the Burges Mous,* Henryson treats the differences in town and country life in some detail (ll. 162–75):

> Esope, myne Authour, makis mentioun
> Of twa myis, and thay wer Sisteris deir,
> Of quham the eldest dwelt in ane Borous toun,
> The uther wynnit uponland weill neir;
> Soliter, quhyle under busk, quhyle under breir,
> Quhilis in the corne, and uther mennis skaith,
> As outlawis dois, and levis on their waith.
>
> This rurall mous in to the wynter tyde,
> Had hunger, cauld, and tholit grit distress;
> The uther Mous, that in the Burgh can byde,
> Was Gild brother and made ane fre Burges;
> Toll fre als, but custom mair or les,
> And fredome had to ga quhair ever scho list,
> Amang the cheis in Ark, and meill in kist.

The description of the country Mouse living the life of an outlaw has some significance for the poet's contemporaries since, although every man was supposed to have a lord, many had been forced to wander at large, taking advantage of the general amnesties decreed during the frequent fairs and festivals held by the burghs.[2]

The vastly superior status of the town Mouse, who was a guild

---

[1] The best treatment of the subject may be found in I. F. Grant, *The Social and Economic Development of Scotland before 1603, passim.*

[2] An old law of King David I states that anyone without a lord must find one within fifteen days or be punished. Cf. I. F. Grant, *Social and Economic Development,* p. 80. For an act of parliament against idlers, cf. P. H. Brown, *Scotland before 1700,* p. 22.

brother and who lived in a borough town without great or small taxes, is worthy of comment. There were two classes of free burgesses in the towns: the craftsmen and the merchants, and although both had their guilds, the merchants were by far the more powerful of the two.[3] The merchants carried on Scotland's commerce, which consisted largely of the exportation of raw materials and the importation of manufactured commodities, paying rent for their land and taxes upon imports and exports. In special cases, the king, who was the immediate landlord of the burghs, granted exemption from taxes in order to encourage the merchants to travel.[4] It is clear that Henryson's town Mouse enjoys the special privileges of a merchant, for she is not only exempt from taxes but also free to travel wherever she wishes.

The poet describes the dwelling and diet of the country Mouse in detail (ll. 197–207):

> As I hard say, it was ane sober wane,
> Off fog & farne ffull febilie wes maid,
> Ane sillie scheill under ane steidfast stane,
> Off quhilk the entres wes not hie nor braid.
> And in the samin thay went but mair abaid,
> Without fyre or candill birnand bricht,
> For comonly sic pykeris luffis not lycht.
>
> Quhen thay wer lugit thus, thir sely Myse,
> The youngest sister into hir butterie glyde,
> And brocht furth nuttis, & candill in steid off spyce;
> Giff this wes gude ffair I do it on thame besyde.

The simple hovel of the country Mouse, feebly made of moss and fern, with an entrance neither high nor broad, is built on the same humble scale as the dwellings of the Scottish rural folk. Aeneas

---

[3] Cf. I. F. Grant, *Social and Economic Development*, pp. 135, 382 ff.

[4] Cf. *ibid.*, p. 133. The merchants sometimes became very wealthy, lent money to the king, and married their children to the nobility. *Ibid.*, p. 382.

Sylvius (Pope Pius II), who visited Scotland in the reign of James I, says that the houses were built without lime, with roofs of turf, and doors of the hide of oxen.[5] Froissart, in the days of David II, indicates that it took three days to build a rural hut, providing the builder had five or six poles, and boughs to cover it.[6]

The town Mouse objects to the food placed before her (ll. 218–24):

> "My fair sister" (quod scho), "have me excusit.
> This rude dyat and I can not accord.
> To tender meit my stomok is ay usit,
> For quhylis I fair alsweill as ony Lord.
> Thir wydderit peis, and nuttis, or they be bord,
> Will brek my teith, and mak my wame fful sklender,
> Quhilk wes before usit to meitis tender."

This country fare of nuts and withered peas is typical of the times. Wheat was uncommon, and although an occasional crop of peas or beans was planted, the principal crops were barley and oats.[7]

The living conditions of the town Mouse form a great contrast to the "rude dyat" of the country Mouse (ll. 260–73, 281–87):

> Not fer fra thyne unto ane worthie Wane,
> This Burges brocht thame sone quhare thay suld be.
> Without God speid thair herberie wes tane,
> In to ane spence with vittell grit plentie;
> Baith Cheis and Butter upon thair skelfis hie,
> And flesche and fische aneuch, baith fresche and salt,
> And sekkis full off meill and eik off malt.
>
> Eftir quhen thay disposit wer to dyne,
> Withowtin grace thay wesche and went to meit,
> With all coursis that Cukis culd devyne,
> Muttoun and beif, strikin in tailyeis greit.

[5] Pii Secundi, *Commentarii Rerum Memorabilium*, p. 4.

[6] *The Chronicle of Froissart*, IV, 23.

[7] I. F. Grant, *Social and Economic Development*, pp. 97 ff. Aeneas Sylvius observes that the common people had little bread. Cf. Pii Secundi, *op. cit.*, p. 4.

Ane Lordis fair thus couth thay counterfeit,
Except ane thing, thay drank the watter cleir
In steid off wyne, bot yit thay maid gude cheir.

. . . . .

Till eik thair cheir ane subcharge furth scho brocht,
Ane plait off grottis, and ane dische full off meill;
Thraf cakkis als I trow scho spairit nocht,
Aboundantlie about hir for to deill.
[And mane full fyne] scho brocht in steid off geill,
And ane quhyte candill out off ane coffer stall,
In steid off spyce to gust thair mouth withall.

In the larder of the town house, the mice find cheese and butter on the shelves, meat and fish (both fresh and salted), and sacks of meal and malt. They dine on mutton and beef, unleavened cakes, and fine bread. The substitution of a candle for spice is apparently a concession to rodent taste.[8]

Henryson does not describe the town house beyond referring to it as a "worthie Wane." [9] Excellent houses existed in Scotland at this date, however, for Pedro de Ayala, the Spanish ambassador to the court of James IV, says that the houses are built of hewn stone and provided with excellent "doors, glass windows, and a great number of chimneys." He adds that "all the furniture that is used in Italy, Spain, and France is to be found in their dwellings." [10] In

---

[8] A dietary for the professors and students of Glasgow University, in the year 1602, offers a comparison. On meat days, the faculty had soup with wheaten bread in it, ale, and cold meat for breakfast;' meat, bread, fowl, and ale for lunch; and "something equivalent" for supper. The students had soup, oaten bread, and ale for breakfast; bread, kale, meat, and ale for lunch; and the same for supper. Cf. I. F. Grant, *Social and Economic Development*, p. 556.

[9] Henryson mentions a "parraling" (l. 337) behind which the country mouse crawls to escape the cat. It may be a partition wall (cf. *NED*, "parpen"). I. F. Grant, however, in her school text, *Everyday Life in Old Scotland*, pp. 99, 103, says that a parraling is a piece of tapestry hung on a wall, usually behind the raised platform upon which the lord and his guests sat at mealtime. This platform, she adds, was located at one end of the great hall which was generally located on the second floor and served as a dining room for the whole household.

[10] *Calendar of Letters . . . between England and Spain*, I, 174.

1498, Andrea Tevisano, the Venetian ambassador to the English court, relates that the Scottish nobility have excellent houses built in the Italian manner of "hewn stone or brick, with magnificent rooms, halls, doors, galleries, chimneys, and windows." [11]

Elsewhere in the *Fables,* Henryson illustrates the position of a farmer in fifteenth-century Scotland. The cultivation of the land was a factor of prime importance in the economic life of fifteenth-century Scotland.[12] Speaking of the more prosperous farmers, John Major observes: "The farmers rent their land from the lords, but cultivate it by means of their servants, and not with their own hands." [13] These subtenants of the farmers were known as "cottars" or "laborers." [14]

With the pictorial sense of a Brueghel, Henryson describes these laborers at work in his *Preiching of the Swallow* (ll. 1720–26):

> Moving thusgait, grit myrth I tuke in mynd,
> Off lauboraris to se the besines,
> Sum makand dyke, and sum the pleuch can wynd,
> Sum sawand seidis fast ffrome place to place,

---

[11] *A Relation . . . of the Island of England . . . about 1500* (London, 1847), p. 15. It should be remembered that Andrea never visited Scotland himself, but speaks on the strength of information derived from Pedro de Ayala, who had some reason to paint a fine picture of Scotland.

[12] Cf. I. F. Grant, *Everyday Life,* p. 295; R. W. Cochran-Patrick, *Mediaeval Scotland,* pp. 1–29. Feudalism characterized the economic structure of the country, and the possession of land directly affected the relations of the crown, church, nobility, and commons. Land was not only the main source of revenue (in 1471, the crown rents constituted two-thirds of the total revenue), but also the source of manpower, security of possessions, and the preservation of life and limb. Cf. I. F. Grant, *op. cit.,* p. 213.

[13] *A History of Greater Britain . . . by John Major,* p. 47.

[14] Cf. I. F. Grant, *Everyday Life,* p. 295. There was a uniform tribal system of cultivating the land in Scotland at this time, whereby the land was divided into an "outfield" used for pasture and an "infield" used for planting. *Ibid.,* pp. 96–97. The customary unit of land was a "plough-gate," and it was worked in common by eight tenants, each owning an "ox-gate," and each contributing one animal to the common plough. The plough-gate consisted of about 104 acres, and it was the equivalent of the "forty-shilling" land upon which taxation and parliamentary representation came to be based. *Ibid.,* p. 45.

> The Harrowis hoppand in the saweris trace:
> It wes grit Joy to him that luifit corne,
> To se thame laubour, baith at evin and morne.

This scene, in which some laborers are engaged in making a wall, others guiding the plough, and still others sowing seed, while the harrow hops along at the sower's heels, illustrates the practice of communal farming.

In a description of the cultivation of the land during this period, Pedro de Ayala confirms and amplifies the poet's scene:

The corn is very good, but they do not produce as much as they might, because they do not cultivate the land. Their method is the following: they plough the land only once when it has grass on it, which is high as a man, then they sow the corn, and cover it by means of a harrow, which makes the land even again. Nothing more is done till they cut the corn. I have seen the straw stand so high after the harvest, that it reached to my girdle.[15]

A hint of the primitive methods with which agriculture was carried on is to be found in Pedro's remark that after planting, nothing more is done until the corn is cut, for drainage and rotation of crops were virtually unknown.[16]

In his fable, *The Taill of the Foxe, that begylit the Wolf, in the schadow of the Mone,* Henryson gives a less happy and more detailed description of the conditions under which the peasants worked (ll. 2232–43, 2252–54):

> Thair wes ane Husband, quhilk had ane pleuch to steir.
> His use wes ay in morning to ryse air;
> Sa happinnit him in streiking tyme of yeir
> Airlie in the morning to follow ffurth his feir,
> Unto the pleuch, bot his gadman and he;
> His stottis he straucht with "Benedicte."
>
> The Caller cryit: "how, haik, upon hicht;
> Hald draucht, my dowis;" syne broddit thame fful sair.

---

[15] *Calendar of Letters,* I, 172.   [16] Cf. I. F. Grant, *Everyday Life,* p. 80.

> The Oxin wes unusit, young and licht,
> And ffor fersnes thay couth the fur fforfair.
> The Husband than woxe angrie as ane hair,
> Syne cryit, and caist his Patill and grit stanis
>
> .   .   .   .   .
>
> The Oxin waxit mair reullie at the last;
> Syne efter thay lousit, ffra that it worthit weill lait;
> The Husband hamewart with his cattell past.

Although the difficulties that beset the husbandman in this passage
may have been heightened for poetic purposes, Henryson is describing
something very real to his contemporaries. Farm implements in this
period were of the crudest type. The cumbersome, heavy ploughs
were made of wood, to which the earth clung so tenaciously during
ploughing that the ploughman was often forced to stop in order
to scrape it off with his "patill," or ploughstaff.[17] The poet says that
the skittish oxen spoiled the furrow and enraged the husbandman,
but it must have been difficult to manage a straight furrow under
any circumstances; eight and even twelve oxen were sometimes required to pull this type of plough, and the assistance of a "gadman"
or goadsman to keep the oxen moving was a necessity.[18]

Henryson also describes the sad fate of the peasant. In his *moralitas*
to the *Taill of the Wolf and the Lamb,* he speaks at length of the
injustices caused by "mychtie men" and "men of heritage, as Lordis,"
who oppress the poor husbandman (ll. 2728–34, 2742–55):

> Ane uther kynd of Wolfis Ravenous,
> Ar mychtie men, haifand full grit plentie,
> Quhilkis ar sa gredie and sa covetous,
> Thay will not thoill the pure in pece to be,
> Suppois he and his houshald baith suld de
> For falt of fude, thairof thay gif na rak,
> Bot over his heid his mailling will thay tak.
>
> .   .   .   .   .

[17] Cf. G. G. Smith, ed., *Poems of* . . . *Henryson,* I, 34.
[18] Cf. I. F. Grant, *Everyday Life,* pp. 80 ff.

The thrid Wolf ar men of heritage,
As Lordis that hes land be Goddis lane,
And settis to the Mailleris ane Village,
And for ane tyme Gressome payit and tane;
Syne vexis him, or half his terme be gane,
With pykit querrelis for to mak him fane
To flit, or pay his Gressome new agane.

His hors, his Meir, he man len to the Laird,
To drug and draw in Court or in Cariage;
His servand or his self may not be spaird
To swing and sweit, withoutin Meit or wage.
Thus how he standis in labour and bondage,
That scantlie may he purches by his maill,
To leve upon dry breid and watter caill.

Contemporary evidence supports the poet's statement that mighty men seize the farms of poor men, while lords of inherited estates rent out pasturage and then, on the pretext of a quarrel, force the farmer to flee although he has paid his rental. Thus, John Major says of the country folk: "They have no permanent holdings, but hired only, or in lease for four or five years, at the pleasure of the lord of the soil; therefore do they not dare to build good houses, though stones abound." [19] The proportion of short leases in this period was also very high, although the duration varied, and it was customary to demand a "gressome," the equivalent of a year's rent, at the beginning or at the renewal of a lease.[20] This rental fell to the landlord upon eviction of the tenant. Numerous acts were passed by parliament to protect the poor farmers by specifying that tenants should be evicted lawfully with due notice and be allowed to remain upon the land until the expiration of their leases, but the very number and repetition of these acts proves that they were ineffective.[21]

[19] Cf. *A History of Greater Britain*, pp. 30–31.
[20] Cf. I. F. Grant, *Social and Economic Development*, p. 225. Also *NED*, "gersum."
[21] Evictions were so common that they interfered with holidays, and an act of parliament in 1469 decreed that evictions should be postponed until three days after

In a strictly feudal economy, the peasant is chained to the soil, thus ensuring the payment of his feudal services. Such an arrangement, which could prove mutually advantageous, one should suppose the feudal lords would be especially interested in maintaining. Yet Henryson tells us that the nobles were evicting the peasants by force. In point of fact, the transition from a feudal to a mercantile economy in the poet's day must have been further advanced than is usually remarked, and the trend from arable land to pasturage must have already commenced. Henryson mentions the trade with Flanders elsewhere, one of the causes of this trend, for the export of wool to the Low Countries was becoming so lucrative that the feudal lords were forcibly evicting the peasants in order to enclose more land for pasturage. Thus, the decline of feudalism was accelerated by the activities of the feudal lords, while the peasant was more frequently and ruthlessly dispossessed.

Henryson's allusions to the farmer are detailed and discerning. The poet describes the rough diet and rude dwellings of the poor Scots who formed the basis of the feudal pyramid, and he had observed with care and pleasure the ploughing and planting of the fields. The poet also was cognizant of the various methods by which the feudal lords harassed the peasants. Although feudalism was doomed and the liberation of the farmer from the soil was a necessary step in the development of a mercantile economy, the path of the transition was beset with many injustices, and Henryson describes them in great detail. In an age when the peasantry is not even mentioned by most authors, Henryson's comments are both unusual and extensive. The poet's attitude toward these facts will be discussed in Chapter VII.

In the socio-economic background of Henryson's day there is the further problem of health and sanitation, a subject upon which the

---

festivals. *Ibid.*, p. 255. There are many records of tenants stripped of their property to satisfy a debt of the landlord. *Ibid.*, p. 257.

poet's references to leprosy have a considerable bearing. This disease was common in Scotland long before and after the poet flourished. The first leper-house north of the Tweed was founded in 1177, and Robert the Bruce died of the disease in 1329 and was buried at Dunfermline. Unlike England, where leprosy reached its peak about the twelfth century and had nearly died out by the fifteenth,[22] Scotland was crowded with lepers until a relatively late date, the disease lingering on in the northern part of the country until the end of the eighteenth century.[23]

In 1427, the Scottish parliament decreed that lepers could enter the burghs three times a week only, and not at all if a fair or market were being held; lepers were also forbidden to beg in kirk or kirkyard or any other place in town, and were ordered to stay outside the burghs and beg either at their own hospitals or at the town gate.[24] In the light of these decrees, we can see why Henryson in his *Testament of Cresseid* set the vivid scene of the lepers swarming around the returning troops of Troilus, shaking their cups and begging for alms (ll. 484 ff.), outside the walls of Troy. Leper hospitals were frequently located outside of the towns,[25] and, as has already been noted, when the poet says that Calchas opened a secret gate and conveyed his daughter to a village half a mile away, leaving her at the spital-house (ll. 388–91), he may be employing details which he had observed in the town of Dunfermline.[26]

Besides being strictly segregated, the lepers were also sadly neglected. The Scottish leper-houses in particular were poorly or not at all endowed, and the lepers were forced to depend almost entirely upon begging. There are many references in the *Testament* to Cresseid's "cop," or begging bowl, and her "clapper," or wooden

---

[22] Cf. R. M. Clay, *The Mediaeval Hospitals of England*, pp. 37 ff.
[23] Cf. P. H. Brown, *Scotland before 1700 from Contemporary Documents*, pp. 199–200.
[24] *Ibid.*, pp. 23–24.   [25] Cf. R. M. Clay, *op. cit.*, pp. xix ff.
[26] Cf. E. Henderson, ed., *Annals of Dunfermline*, pp. 169–70, and *supra*, p. 12, note 39.

rattle.[27] When the poet says that there was nothing for Cresseid to do but to go forth with the lepers (ll. 482–83)

> Fra place to place, quhill cauld and hounger sair
> Compellit hir to be ane rank beggair,

he is describing the fate of lepers in his day. Since it was customary to send spoiled pork or salmon to the lepers,[28] Cresseid's plea, "sum meit for cheritie me send to leif upon" (ll. 383–84), as well as Henryson's description of the "uncouth fair" (l. 403), has some foundation in fact.[29]

The poet's description of Cresseid's symptoms is remarkably detailed. Saturn announces (ll. 316–18):

> "I change thy mirth into Melancholy,
> Quhilk is the Mother of all pensivenes;
> Thy Moisture and thy heit in cald and dry . . ."

To this Cynthia adds (ll. 334–40);

> "Fra heit of bodie I the now depryve,
> And to thy seiknes sal be na recure,
> Bot in dolour thy dayis to Indure.
>
> "Thy Cristall Ene minglit with blude I mak,
> Thy voice sa cleir, unplesand hoir and hace,
> Thy lustie lyre ouirspred with spottis blak,
> And lumpis haw appeirand in thy face . . ."

Later, Cresseid says (ll. 438–51);

> "This Lipper Ludge tak for thy burelie Bour.
> And for thy Bed tak now ane bunche of stro,
> For waillit Wyne, and Meitis thou had tho,

---

[27] Cf. R. M. Clay, *op. cit.,* pp. 68–69, and the *Testament,* ll. 343, 387, 442, 492, 579.

[28] Cf. G. G. Coulton, *Medieval Panorama,* pp. 455–56.

[29] Cf. J. Parr, "Cresseid's Leprosy Again," *MLN,* LX (November, 1945), 491, where it is suggested that Cresseid's poor diet is dictated by the medical "regimen for elephantiasis." The suggestion is valuable, but it might be added that it runs counter to the poet's aim of emphasizing the utter desertion of Cresseid.

Tak mowlit Breid, Peirrie and Ceder sour;
Bot Cop and Clapper, now is all ago.

"My cleir voice, and courtlie carrolling,
Quhair I was wont with Ladyis for to sing,
Is rawk as Ruik, full hiddeous hoir and hace,
My plesand port all utheris precelling:
Of lustiness I was hald maist conding.
Now is deformit the Figour of my face,
To luik on it, na Leid now lyking hes:
Sowpit in syte, I say with sair siching,
Ludgeit amang the Lipper Leid allace."

This description of the symptoms of leprosy is so accurate that the physician, Sir J. Y. Simpson, cited it as proof that cases of Greek elephantiasis existed in Scotland just as they are known to have existed on the Continent. Dr. Simpson says:

The particular symptoms which he makes Saturn invoke upon Cresseid, to transform her into a Leper, are exactly the most marked symptoms of Greek elephantiasis. . . . In this remarkable passage, those more striking symptoms, the swellings, lumps, or livid tubercles on the face, the morbid alteration of the voice and skin, and that turgid and injected appearance of the eye, which Dr Good has given as one of his characteristic symptoms of the *genus* Elephantiasis, are all tersely, yet accurately described.

In passages subsequent to that which I have quoted [ll. 337–43], Henryson reiterates some of the more prominent symptoms. Thus, the hopeless Cresseid describes what is elsewhere termed "hir uglye lipper face, the whilk before was quhite (white) as Lilie flour," as "deformed the figour;" and again also she describes and laments the characteristic morbid change in the voice . . .[30]

In the poet's day, leprosy was classified according to four types: *leonina, elephantina, alopica,* and *tyria,* and of these types, elephantiasis was regarded (and still is) as the least curable.[31] Henryson states several times in the *Testament* that there was "na recure" for

[30] J. Y. Simpson, "Antiquarian Notices of Leprosy and Leper Hospitals in Scotland and England," *Edinburgh Medical and Surgical Journal,* LVII (1842), 139–40.
[31] *Ibid.,* p. 313.

Cresseid.[32] Further, since the duty of inspecting and reporting lepers often devolved upon the parish priest, who frequently became something of an expert on the subject,[33] there may be a connection between this fact and the poet's statement that Calchas, who was a priest, looked upon his daughter's face and "knew weill that thair was na succour to hir seiknes" (ll. 376–77). Again, Cresseid's desire not to be known and her request to be taken secretly to the leper-house (ll. 380–82) are in keeping with a frequently noted symptom of leprosy, the desire to avoid society.[34]

Henryson's presentation of Cresseid's leprosy also illustrates the practice of astrology and astrological medicine, a subject which will be discussed more fully in connection with the planet portraits. The choice of the planets Saturn and Cynthia to judge Cresseid is not accidental; whereas the complexion of Cresseid's former goddess, Venus, is hot and moist, and Cresseid is described as having had a sanguine temperament composed of these qualities,[35] the complexion of Saturn is cold and dry, or melancholic, the qualities conferred upon Cresseid and the qualities commonly supposed to be the cause of Greek elephantiasis.[36] Further, Cresseid is afflicted with the disease between noon and suppertime, the third set of hours when melancholy rules,[37] and by Saturn and Cynthia, who have jurisdiction over leprosy.[38]

We may reasonably conclude that Henryson had not only observed lepers at first hand, but also was sufficiently acquainted with the

---

[32] *Testament*, ll. 335, 376, 411, 455.   [33] Cf. R. M. Clay, *op. cit.*, p. 59.

[34] Cf. H. P. Cholmeley, ed., *John of Gaddesden and the Rosa Medicinae*, p. 45.

[35] Cf. *Testament*, ll. 318, 334.

[36] Cf. Bartholomaeus Anglicus, *De proprietatibus rerum*, tr. J. Trevisa, Bk. VII, chap. lxv; and W. C. Curry, *Chaucer and the Mediaeval Sciences*, pp. 41 ff.

[37] *Ibid.*, p. 14.

[38] Cf. W. Lilly, *Christian Astrology*, p. 59. Cf. further, J. Parr, *op. cit.*, pp. 487–88, where additional examples are cited. Parr concludes that Cresseid's symptoms are found in medical treatises and implies that Henryson might have avoided the firsthand observation of such facts—an implication which may overlook the wide prevalence of the disease and the realistic and inquiring spirit of the poet.

astrological medicine of his day to select the most formidable type of leprosy, thus making Cresseid's fate appear even more irrevocable. In so doing, the poet added an element to the Troilus legend which bids fair to be permanent. The general adoption of this detail by later authors, including Shakespeare and Dryden, testifies to its poetic justice.

Chapter IV

HENRYSON AND CHAUCER

*A*LTHOUGH ROBERT HENRYSON stands highest among all of Chaucer's disciples according to one critic,[1] and although the poet's *Testament of Cresseid* is the best of all poems in the post-Chaucerian school according to another,[2] scholars have found no time to investigate the nature of the Scot's obligation to his master. The following remarks are directed toward a better understanding of the relationship of the two poets and a more accurate evaluation of the later poet's accomplishment.

I

A comparison of the characters in Chaucer's *Troilus and Criseyde* with those that reappear in Henryson's sequel, *The Testament of Cresseid,* is instructive. Four of Chaucer's characters occur in the *Testament:* Diomede, Troilus, Calchas, and Cresseid.[3] There is no characterization of Diomede in the *Testament* beyond that implied in the following lines (ll. 71–75):

> Quhen Diomeid had all his appetyte,
> And mair, fulfillit of this fair Ladie,
> Upon ane uther he set his haill delyte
> And send to hir ane Lybell of repudie,[4]
> And hir excludit fra his companie.

[1] Aldous Huxley, *Essays New and Old*, p. 272.
[2] G. G. Coulton, *Medieval Panorama*, p. 589.
[3] Henryson does not mention Pandarus, probably because the sequel takes up the story long after Pandarus has played his part in bringing the two lovers together.
[4] "Lybell of repudie," i.e., *libellum repudii,* a bill of divorcement. Cf. G. G. Smith, ed., *Poems of . . . Henryson*, I, 45, note to line 74.

Diomede's desertion of Cresseid is in keeping with Chaucer's characterization of "this sodein Diomede" (V, 1024).[5] Nevertheless, it is
with a distinct shock that the reader of Chaucer's poem becomes
aware of Diomede's brutal act in the *Testament*. The contrast with
Criseyde's desperate resolution to be true to Diomede in the *Troilus
and Criseyde* (V, 1071) is striking, since Henryson denies her the
opportunity and tells us shortly that she became a whore (ll. 77, 80–
83).

In the *Testament,* Troilus plays the part of that colorless abstrac-
tion, the perfect gentleman, a part derived in great measure from
Chaucer.[6] In her lament, Cresseid speaks of Troilus (ll. 547–48,
554–57):

> "Thy lufe, thy lawtie, and thy gentilnes,
> I countit small in my prosperitie
>
> .   .   .   .   .
>
> "For lufe,[7] of me thou keipt gude continence,
> Honest and chaist in conversatioun.
> Of all wemen protectour and defence
> Thou was, and helpit thair opinioun."

These characteristics are more or less the conventional courtly love
attributes found in an expanded form in Chaucer.[8] Yet there is a
significant change of emphasis: Henryson nowhere refers to the

---

[5] Professor Tatlock speaks persuasively of Diomede's "obvious experience" and his
"cool technique as seducer," dismissing his avowal of lifelong fidelity to Criseyde as
pretense and adding that "such is his cool-headedness in both poets that Robert Henryson's *Testament of Cresseid* shows the inevitable course of events in his tiring of her
and abandoning her." J. S. P. Tatlock, "The People in Chaucer's *Troilus*," *PMLA*,
LVI (March, 1941), 94–95.

[6] In the *Testament*, Troilus is thrice called true (ll. 546, 553, 560), twice noble (ll.
132, 495), twice worthy (ll. 42, 485), and once gentle and free (l. 536). These adjectives are found for the most part in Chaucer: cf. *Tr*, V, 831 (trewe); V, 1056, 1075
(gentileste); II, 319 (noble), *et passim*.

[7] The comma after "lufe" seems not only unnecessary but also confusing.

[8] Cf. *Tr*, III, 266 (protect name); III, 286 (keep tongue); III, 427 (self-control); III,
1804–6 (flee vices), *et passim*.

virtue of "secrecy" as Chaucer does,[9] but he does speak of "gude continence" (l. 554), which Chaucer does not mention.[10] This difference in emphasis becomes more noticeable when the Scot contrasts the chaste virtues of Troilus with the "Lustis Lecherous" and "fleschelie foull affectioun" of Cresseid (ll. 558–59), a contrast which Chaucer avoids. In the *Testament,* Troilus manifests symptoms common to courtly love (ll. 512–18), but they are inclined to be the symptoms typical of romantic love in any age. The net effect of Henryson's treatment of the character of Troilus is merely to make him less the typical courtly lover and more the typical romantic lover.[11]

Henryson modifies the character of Calchas considerably. In the *Testament,* Calchas is the priest of Venus, not of Apollo as in the *Troilus and Criseyde.* Since Cresseid's horrible fate is the result of her blasphemy of Venus and Cupid, this innovation adds to the dramatic unity of the *Testament.* For apparently similar reasons, Henryson institutes a fundamental change by making Calchas and his daughter mutually sympathetic. Thus, after her desertion by Diomede, Cresseid is received kindly by her father (ll. 103–5):

> Quod Calchas, "douchter, weip thou not thairfoir;
> Peraventure all cummis for the best;
> Welcum to me, thou art full deir ane Gest."

Later, when Calchas learns that his daughter has become a leper, he is genuinely concerned (ll. 372–78):

> He luikit on hir uglye Lipper face,
> The quhilk befor was quhyte as Lillie flour,
> Wringand his handis oftymes he said allace
> That he had levit to se that wofull hour,
> For he knew weill that thair was na succour
> To hir seiknes, and that dowblit his pane.
> Thus was thair cair aneuch betuix thame twane.

---

[9] *Tr,* III, 286, 294 ff.

[10] Chaucer does speak of "goode governaunce" (*Tr,* III, 427), which may be glossed as self-control or good demeanor.

[11] Cf. J. S. P. Tatlock, "The People in Chaucer's *Troilus,*" pp. 92–93.

Upon Cresseid's decision to hide herself in a leper colony, she is taken there secretly by Calchas, who "daylie sent hir part of his Almous" (l. 392).

The extent to which Henryson is an innovator can be appreciated only in the light of the intense dislike which exists between Calchas and Criseyde in Chaucer,[12] and the traditional antipathy between the two found in earlier versions of the story.[13] The poet makes the change in order to increase the pathos of Cresseid's downfall. Thus Cresseid, having just discovered that the gods have afflicted her with a foul disease, is summoned gaily by her unknowing father (ll. 358–64):

> Be this was said ane Chyld come fra the Hall
> To warne Cresseid the Supper was reddy,
> First knokkit at the dure, and syne culd call:
> "Madame your Father biddis yow cum in hy.
> He hes mervell sa long on grouf ye ly,
> And sayis your prayers bene to lang sum deill:
> The goddis wait all your Intent full weill."

The dramatic irony of Calchas' playful request that Cresseid stop praying, since the gods know all her thoughts very well, is furthered

---

[12] In the *Tr*, when Criseyde learns of the exchange of prisoners, Chaucer says that she "of hire fader roughte . . . right nought, ne whan he deyde" (IV, 667–68); on leaving for the Greek camp, she suggests tricking her father by the promise of gold; she speaks of Calchas as "ful of coveytise" (IV, 1369), as having a "coward herte" (IV, 1409), and as desiring her return only because of public opinion (IV, 1338 ff.). Cf. J. S. P. Tatlock, "The People in Chaucer's *Troilus*," p. 102.

[13] From Benoit on, what may be termed the "recrimination scene" appears in most of the versions of the Troilus story. This scene usually occurs after the exchange of prisoners, and it consists of Criseyde's reproaching her father for his treason to the Trojans while Calchas attempts to justify himself. Cf. L. Constans, ed., *Le Roman de Troie*, II, 323–25; N. E. Griffin, ed., *Guido de Columnis historia destructionis Troiae*, pp. 165–66; G. A. Panton and D. Donaldson, eds., *The "Gest Hystoriale" of the Destruction of Troy*, pp. 263–65; and H. O. Sommer, ed., *The Recuyell of the Historyes of Troye*, II, 604–5. The *Laud Troy Book* omits this scene, and it is softened in the *Filostrato*, although Boccaccio invents the plot to deceive Calchas which Chaucer adopts. Cf. N. E. Griffin and A. B. Myrick, eds., *The Filostrato of Giovanni Boccaccio*, pp. 325, 331, 353, 363, 455.

by the fact of their mutual affection. Glancing in the mirror at her now loathsome face, Cresseid cannot help being struck by the mockery of her father's loving summons.

Henryson simplifies the character of Cresseid. Like his predecessor, the Scot declares his sympathy with his heroine, for Chaucer had written (V, 1095–99):

> Hire name, allas! is punysshed so wide,
> That for hire gilt it oughte ynough suffise.
> And if I myghte excuse hire any wise,
> For she so sory was for hire untrouthe,
> Iwis, I wolde excuse hire yet for routhe.

In the same vein and, indeed, with a few of the same words, Henryson writes (ll. 84–91):

> I have pietie thou suld fall sic mischance.

> Yit nevertheless quhat ever men deme or say
> In scornefull langage of thy brukkilnes,
> I sall excuse, als far furth as I may,
> Thy womanheid, thy wisdome and fairnes;
> The quhilk Fortoun hes put to sic distres
> As hir pleisit, and nathing throw the gilt
> Of the, throw wickit langage to be spilt.

Henryson goes further than Chaucer in his sympathy for Cresseid: he declares that Fortune is to blame and that Cresseid is guiltless.[14] But neither poet means to question the fact of her infidelity; they simply share a pardonable bias in favor of their heroine.

In another instance, Henryson may be following Chaucer more literally, for the earlier poet has Criseyde prophesy her own fate (V, 1058–62):

> Allas! of me, unto the worldes ende,
> Shal neyther ben ywriten nor ysonge

---

[14] It may be that Henryson, taking Cresseid's guilt and punishment for granted, found it easy to slip into the habit of blaming it all on Fortune, while Chaucer, with Criseyde's fall in progress, could not allow himself such wishful thinking.

No good word, for thise bokes wol me shende.
O, rolled shal I ben on many a tonge!
Throughout the world my belle shal be ronge!

In the *Testament,* the seven planets are called together to doom Cresseid by (ll. 144-45):

Cupide the King ringand ane silver bell,
Quhilk men micht heir fra hevin unto hell.

Thus Criseyde's prophecy comes to pass.

There are other minor parallels between Henryson's and Chaucer's heroines,[15] but in general the Scot is content to take her as he finds her in his predecessor, limiting himself to the simple characterization permitted by his bold change of plot. Troilus lives happily and Cresseid dies miserably. In the course of her downfall, Cresseid asserts herself but once and then in a manner not unworthy of her Chaucerian self. Deserted even by Diomede, she falls to cursing her gods, Venus and Cupid. It is her last independent act, for this blasphemy brings down upon her the wrath of the gods and the punishment of leprosy.[16]

The key to Henryson's variations upon Chaucer's characterizations, except in the case of Calchas where they are made for dramatic purposes, seems to be the Scot's inability or refusal to adopt the elements of courtly morality in Chaucer. The effect of the *Troilus and*

---

[15] In the *Testament,* Cresseid mentions a ring and a brooch which Troilus gave her (ll. 582-84, 589-91). These may be found in the *Troilus and Criseyde* (III, 1368, 1370). There is no precedent in Chaucer, however, for the belt which Henryson mentions (l. 589). It has been suggested that it may refer to a chastity girdle. Cf. H. H. Wood, *The Poems and Fables of Robert Henryson,* p. 258.

[16] Professor Rollins' suggestion that Henryson's treatment of Cresseid "forever damned her as a loose woman" may be misleading. Cf. H. E. Rollins, "The Troilus-Cressida Story from Chaucer to Shakespeare," *PMLA,* XXXIII (1917), 397. Cresseid is liberally damned both before and after Chaucer. Both Benoit and Guido, as well as Boccaccio, condemn her for her infidelity. It is rather in Chaucer and Henryson that the exception occurs. As Professor Tatlock says, "Originally of course this woman is nothing at all except a loose jilt." *Op. cit.,* p. 101. The credit for conceiving of the punishment of leprosy is entirely Henryson's, but this creative detail does not account for Cresseid's degradation.

Criseyde is to show "how infinitely appealing a woman notoriously to become faithless could be," [17] and although Criseyde is probably blameworthy by any moral standard,[18] Chaucer hesitates to judge or condemn her. On the other hand, Henryson's sequel is conceived and written according to the standards of orthodox morality. Aided perhaps by the fact that he was adding a new denouement, Henryson applied his own standards consistently: brutally deserted by Diomede, Cresseid sinks to the level of a prostitute; Troilus is chaste and he is described mainly by those courtly characteristics that are common to romantic love in any age. It is logical, therefore, that the repentant Cresseid should die warning others to beware of infidelity, and that Henryson, unlike Chaucer,[19] should conclude his poem with the exhortation to women not to mingle love with false deception. The *Testament of Cresseid* presents the tragedy of one who is punished not only for the sin of pride, but also for the sin of lust.

II

There are elements of a new plot, or narrative design, in the *Testament* which make the poem an independent dramatic whole. For the purposes of discussion, this plot may be described as a three-fold sequence of contract, crime, and punishment. The contract consists of an agreement between Cresseid and the gods of love (ll. 124–28, 136, 138):

> Upon Venus and Cupide angerly
> Scho cryit out, and said on this same wyse,
> "Allace that ever I maid you Sacrifice.
>
> Ye gave me anis ane devine responsaill
> That I suld be the flour of luif in Troy

. . . . .

[17] Cf. J. S. P. Tatlock, "The People in Chaucer's *Troilus*," p. 101.
[18] Cf. C. S. Lewis, *The Allegory of Love*, p. 184.
[19] In the lines preceding his epilogue, Chaucer concludes: "Beth war of men" (*Tr*, V, 1785), and the implication is that the poet, unable to condemn his heroine, twists the moral into the more acceptable form of a warning to women to beware of men.

> "Ye causit me alwayis understand and trow
> The seid of lufe was sawin in my face,
> And ay grew grene throw your supplie and grace."

Cresseid, in return for the divine promise made by Venus and Cupid that she would always be the flower of love in Troy, had showered devotion upon her chosen gods, only to deplore that devotion when she thinks that they have failed her.[20]

Cresseid's crime, and the immediate cause of her downfall, is her blasphemy of the gods of love. Deserted by Diomede, she feels with some reason that Venus and Cupid have not maintained their part of the bargain (ll. 129-35):

> "Now am I maid ane unworthie outwaill,
> And all in cair translatit is my Joy,
> Quha sall me gyde? quha sall me now convoy
> Sen I fra Diomeid and Nobill Troylus
> Am clene excludit, as abject odious?

> "O fals Cupide, is nane to wyte bot thow,
> And thy Mother, of lufe the blind Goddes!"

Cresseid places the blame squarely upon Cupid and his mother, to whom she refers angrily as the blind goddess of love.[21] These words are termed blasphemy by Cupid when he appears before the court of the gods, and he demands punishment (ll. 274-87):

> "Lo!" (quod Cupide), "quha will blaspheme the name
> Of his awin God, outher in word or deid,
> To all Goddis he dois baith lak and schame,
> And suld have bitter panis to his meid.

This passage must have seemed as incongruous to Henryson as it does to the modern reader.

[20] Cf. *Testament*, ll. 279, 354.

[21] In calling Venus a blind goddess, Cresseid may be adding insult to injury by confusing the time-honored attributes of the two gods. Cupid refers to it later with vehemence (ll. 282-84), indicating that the poet may have used it intentionally. No precedent has been found for Cresseid's statement. In classical literature, Cupid was rarely depicted as blind although he became so later. Cf. E. Panofsky, *Studies in Iconology*, pp. 95-128.

I say this by yone wretchit Cresseid,
The quilk throw me was sum tyme flour of lufe,
Me and my Mother starklie can reprufe.

"Saying of hir greit Infelicitie
I was the caus, and my Mother Venus,
Ane blind Goddes, hir cald, that micht not se,
With sclander and defame Injurious;
Thus hir leving unclene and Lecherous
Scho wald returne on me and my Mother,
To quhome I schew my grace abone all uther."

Later in the poem Cresseid speaks of her "blaspheming" (l. 354) and
her "trespas" (l. 370), while her crime is termed a "dispyte to Cupide"
(l. 304).

Cresseid's punishment is leprosy. Incensed by her blasphemy, Cupid
demands vengeance from the court of the seven planets (ll. 288–94):

"And sen ye ar all sevin deificait,
Participant of devyne sapience,
This greit Injurie done to our hie estait
Me think with pane we suld mak recompence;
Was never to Goddes done sic violence.
Asweill for yow, as for myself I say,
Thairfoir ga help to revenge I yow pray."

Cresseid's punishment follows swiftly (ll. 304–8):

For the dispyte to Cupide scho had done,
And to Venus oppin and manifest,
In all her lyfe with pane to be opprest,
And torment sair, with seiknes Incurabill,
And to all lovers be abhominabill.

Cresseid becomes the opposite of what she once was: not only are
the charms promised by Cupid and Venus withdrawn, but she is
cursed also with a malady that makes any romantic love impossible.
It is a short step to her last, poignant meeting with the unknowing
Troilus and her inglorious death.

There is a distinct possibility that Henryson found the germ for his plot or narrative design in a minor poem of Chaucer's: *Lenvoy de Chaucer a Scogan*. For although isolated elements in the Scot's threefold plot sequence may be found in a variety of sources, Chaucer's piece to Scogan is the only poem I have been able to discover in which the entire sequence occurs intact. In the light of Henryson's profound knowledge of Chaucer elsewhere, the parallel between the *Testament* and *Scogan* seems to be more than a coincidence.

The pertinent lines in *Scogan* are as follows (ll. 1–28, 49):

> Tobroken been the statutz hye in hevene
> That creat were eternally to dure,
> Syth that I see the bryghte goddis sevene
> Mowe wepe and wayle, and passion endure,
> As may in erthe a mortal creature.
> Allas, fro whennes may thys thing procede?
> Of which errour I deye almost for drede.
>
> By word eterne whilom was yshape
> That fro the fyfte sercle, in no manere,
> Ne myghte a drope of teeres doun escape.
> But now so wepith Venus in hir spere
> That with hir teeres she wol drenche us here.
> Allas! Scogan, this is for thyn offence;
> Thow causest this diluge of pestilence.
>
> Hastow not seyd, in blaspheme of the goddes,
> Thurgh pride, or thrugh thy grete rekelnesse,
> Swich thing as in the lawe of love forbode is,
> That, for thy lady sawgh nat thy distresse,
> Therfore thow yave hir up at Michelmesse?
> Allas! Scogan, of olde folk ne yonge
> Was never erst Scogan blamed for his tonge.
>
> Thow drowe in skorn Cupide eke to record
> Of thilke rebel word that thou hast spoken,
> For which he wol no lenger be thy lord.
> And, Scogan, though his bowe be nat broken,

He wol nat with his arwes been ywroken
On the, ne me, ne noon of oure figure;
We shul of him have neyther hurt ne cure

. . . . .

Far-wel, and loke thow never eft Love dyffye.

Here Chaucer is using the sequence of contract, crime, and punishment with humorous intent to describe a trivial incident.

The existence of a contract is evident in the assertion that Cupid "wol no lenger be thy lord." [22] Scogan had been devoted to the gods of love until he found that he was not attaining success in return, for his "lady sawgh nat" his distress. The crime is that Scogan defied "Love" in general, and stated that he gave up his lady at "Michelmesse" in particular.[23] This crime is called "blaspheme of the goddes," an "offence," and "thilke rebel word" which "in the lawe of love forbode is." Scogan's motive, like Cresseid's, is "pride" and "grete rekelnesse," while the effect of the crime is to break the "statutz hye in hevene" (rules of courtly love?), to cause Venus and the "bryghte goddis sevene" to weep, and to drive Cupid to repudiate Scogan "in

---

[22] The idea that the lover must be devoted to his gods is a commonplace. Cf., for example, *The Court of Love* in W. W. Skeat's *Chaucerian and Other Pieces*, p. 417 (ll. 304–7). The idea that the gods must reward the lover, however, although frequently implied, is less frequently stated explicitly. In the *Confessio Amantis*, Procne prays to Cupid and Venus for revenge, citing her own faithfulness, and her prayer is granted. G. C. Macaulay, ed., *The Complete Works of John Gower*, III, 105 ff. This is the usual procedure. A more explicit example may be found in the *Kingis Quair*, where Venus tells the lover to continue in her service, worship her law, and magnify her name, in return for which she will multiply his comforts on earth and give him eternal life with her when he dies. A. Lawson, ed., *The Kingis Quair*, p. 63.

[23] The complaint to the gods of love is very common, although it seldom attains the level of blasphemy so-called and rarely follows a contract or incurs a punishment. In Lydgate's *Complaint of the Black Knight*, for example, the god of love is accused in round terms of a variety of faults, but no punishment of the blasphemer follows. Cf. H. N. MacCracken, ed., *The Minor Poems of John Lydgate*, II, 401 ff. In *The Fall of Princes*, Canace blames Cupid for her fate but is not punished. H. Bergen, ed., *Lydgate's Fall of Princes*, I, 197 ff. Cf. further, G. C. Macaulay, ed., *Works of John Gower*, II, 39 ff. In the *Kingis Quair*, however, James I mentions certain lovers who are unhappy "for dispite." Cf. A. Lawson, ed., *The Kingis Quair*, p. 44.

skorn." The punishment is a "diluge of pestilence," [24] the fact that Cupid will no longer aid Scogan, and the possibility (suggested but denied) that Cupid will take revenge with his bow and arrows.[25]

A few more detailed resemblances between *Scogan* and the *Testament* deserve notice. Scogan's crime is "blaspheme of the goddes," while Cresseid refers to her crime as "blaspheming," a word also used by Cupid; Scogan is blamed "for his tonge" and Cresseid for her "fraward langage"; Chaucer refers to the planets as the "goddis sevene," and Henryson calls them the "Goddes sevin." Cupid plays the active role and Venus plays the passive role in both poems, while all the planets are affected adversely.[26] Finally, Chaucer's ambiguous reference to Scogan as the cause of a "diluge of pestilence," whatever the poet may have meant, is suggestively similar to Cresseid's punishment of leprosy.[27]

[24] This may refer to a contemporary epidemic of the plague or (more likely) heavy rains. Cf. F. N. Robinson, ed., *Complete Works of Chaucer*, pp. 978–79.

[25] The punishment of lovers by the gods, with the implied concept that the gods of love are all-powerful, is very common, although it is not found in the sequence being discussed. Venus takes prompt revenge when annoyed. Cf. *Ars amatoria*, II, 397–98. This mythological commonplace should be distinguished, however, from the example of the medieval goddess of love who punishes her feudal subjects. Cf. Gower's tale of Rosiphelee, in G. C. Macaulay, ed., *Works of John Gower*, II, 334 ff.

[26] The relationship of Cupid and Venus is of interest. In Ovid, the "lascive puer" who is called the "arma manusque meae, mea, nate, potentia" of Venus (*Met*, I, 456; V, 365) became variously related to Venus in later literature. In the *Roman de la Rose*, Venus is the goddess of sensual love as opposed to her son's connection with *l'amour du coeur*. Cf. E. Langlois, ed., *Le Roman de la Rose*, III, 173 ff.; W. A. Neilson, *The Origins and Sources of the Court of Love*, p. 55; and C. S. Lewis, *op. cit.*, p. 121. In the *Confessio Amantis*, Cupid is subordinated to Venus. Cf. W. G. Dodd, *Courtly Love in Chaucer and Gower*, pp. 45–46. In the *Kingis Quair*, the distinction is made that Cupid wounds while Venus cures. Cf. A. Lawson, ed., *The Kingis Quair*, p. 54. In Lydgate's *Complaint of the Black Knight*, Venus and Cupid are referred to as a double diety. Cf. H. N. MacCracken, ed., *Minor Poems of . . . Lydgate*, II, 401. In the *Court of Love*, they are called god and goddess. Cf. W. W. Skeat, *Chaucerian . . . Pieces*, p. 410. The iconology of Cupid is discussed by E. Panofsky, *op. cit.*, pp. 95–128.

[27] A few examples of sickness or pestilence decreed by the gods have been examined, but they offer no sustained analogy to the *Testament*. The fact that Azariah was

It should be added that a minor version of the plot sequence of contract, crime, and punishment occurs in the *Troilus and Criseyde*. The sequence, however, is inverted: Troilus commits the crime of mocking at love and lovers; he is punished by being made to fall desperately in love; and by promising humble devotion to the gods of love, he is granted eventual success.[28] There is no reason to suppose that Henryson was not only aware of but also influenced by either one or both of these passages in Chaucer. For they both contain in small compass several elements which make up the narrative design of the *Testament of Cresseid*.

III

The opening lines of the *Testament of Cresseid* bear an interesting relationship to Chaucer. The Scot calls his poem a "tragedie," i.e., a fall from felicity to misery, and proceeds to introduce his story accordingly (ll. 1–21):

> Ane doolie sessoun to ane cairfull dyte
> Suld correspond, and be equivalent.
> Richt sa it wes quhen I began to wryte
> This tragedie, the wedder richt fervent,
> Quhen Aries, in middis of the Lent,[29]
> Schouris of haill can fra the north discend,
> That scantlie fra the cauld I micht defend.

> Yit nevertheless within myne oratur
> I stude, quhen Titan had his bemis bricht
> Withdrawin doun, and sylit under cure
> And fair Venus, the bewtie of the nicht,

---

made a leper because of his pride is mentioned by Lydgate. Cf. H. Bergen, ed., *Fall of Princes*, II, 649. In the *Fall of Princes*, Lydgate relates how Laodamia's death brings a pestilence upon her murderers. *Ibid.*, 592. The most interesting analogy may be found in Gower's *Confessio Amantis*, in the tale of "criseide, douhter of Crisis," whose rape and abduction by Agamemnon are punished by pestilence. Cf. G. C. Macaulay, ed., *Works of John Gower*, III, 124 ff.

[28] Cf. *Tr*, I, 197–205, 206–9, 526–29, 936–38; II, 522–32, 680–83.

[29] The first week of April; cf. W. W. Skeat, *Chaucerian . . . Pieces*, p. 521.

Uprais, and set unto the west full richt
Hir goldin face in oppositioun
Of God Phebus direct discending doun.

Throw out the glas [30] hir bemis brast sa fair
That I micht se on everie syde me by
The Northin wind had purifyit the Air
And sched the mistie cloudis fra the sky,
The froist freisit, the blastis bitterly
Fra Pole Artick come quhisling loud and schill,
And causit me remufe aganis my will.

By thus introducing his poem with a reference to the time of year and a description of the weather, Henryson is employing a common device in the literature of his times.

The typical elements of this device occur at the opening of the *Roman de la Rose* (ll. 47, 80, 124–25) : [31]

> Qu'en mai estoie, ce sonjoie
>
> . . . . .
>
> Por le tens bel e doucereus
>
> . . . . .
>
> Clere e serie e bele estoit
> La matinee e atempree.

Similar passages occur in the Old French love-visions,[32] in the poems of Chaucer,[33] and in post-Chaucerian poems.[34] In general, the device

[30] The poet was probably acquainted with glass windows. Cf. G. G. Smith, ed., *Poems of . . . Henryson,* I, 44.

[31] E. Langlois, ed., *Le Roman de la Rose,* II, 3, 5, 7. Cf. Chaucer's *Romaunt,* ll. 51, 84, 130–31.

[32] Cf. W. O. Sypherd *Studies in Chaucer's Hous of Fame,* pp. 1–6. Professor Sypherd finds the device in five of the seven poems he analyzes, and establishes the fact that it is conventional.

[33] Cf. *BD,* ll. 291, 341–42 (month of May, temperate weather); *PF,* ll. 210, 204–5 (clear day, temperate air); *LGW,* ll. 36, 108, 176 (month of May).

[34] Cf. *The Complaint of the Black Knight* (H. N. MacCracken, ed., *Minor Poems of . . . Lydgate,* II, 382); *The Cuckoo and the Nightingale* (W. W. Skeat, *Chaucerian . . . Pieces,* pp. 347 ff.); A. Lawson, ed., *The Kingis Quair,* pp. 27, 35; and the *Confessio Amantis* (G. C. Macaulay, ed., *Works of John Gower,* II, 38). Cf. further *The Flower and the Leaf* (W. W. Skeat, *Chaucerian . . . Pieces,* p. 361); *Reson and*

consists of a description of a pleasant day in May which occurs within a vision or dream after the poet has fallen asleep.

Henryson's adaptation of the device forms a sharp contrast. The season is wintry, he says, to correspond with the mood of a sorrowful poem, and he describes a hailstorm from the north in impressive detail. By so doing, the poet parallels the appropriateness of a May morning to a love-vision. Further, Henryson discards the dream framework and speaks in terms of a present experience with attention to the details of his immediate surroundings. He is standing within his oratory as Venus with her "goldin face" shines "throw out the glas," and looking outside, he sees that the wind has "purifyit the Air and sched the mistie cloudis fra the sky." These details appear to be taken from Chaucer's *Book of the Duchess* (ll. 335-38, 340, 343):

> My windowes were shette echon,
> And throgh the glas the sonne shon
> Upon my bed with bryghte bemes,
> With many glade gilde stremes
>
> .   .   .   .   .
>
> Blew, bryght, clere was the ayr
>
> .   .   .   .   .
>
> Ne in al the welken was no clowde.

Both poets describe themselves as indoors, gazing out upon the clear air and cloudless sky, through a glass window which is admitting bright beams of light.

There is no known model for Chaucer's lines and, so far as I have been able to ascertain, Henryson could not have hit upon a similar description elsewhere.[35] In the course, then, of adapting the May-day

---

Sensuallyte (E. Sieper, ed., *Lydgate's Reson and Sensuallyte,* p. 3); *The Floure of Curtesye* (H. N. MacCracken, ed., *Minor Poems of . . . Lydgate,* II, 410); and the *Temple of Glas* (J. Schick, ed., *Lydgate's Temple of Glas,* p. 1).

[35] In general, the poet's surroundings are not described until after he thinks he is awake and goes into some grove or meadow. So in *Le Roman de la Rose,* the *Com-*

device to a "cairfull dyte" with suitably wintry weather, Henryson appears to have gone to the *Book of the Duchess* for a few details. The net result is a fitting and effective introduction to his poem.

IV

The attitudes of Chaucer and Henryson toward courtly love afford an interesting comparison and contrast. In the *Troilus and Criseyde,* Chaucer wrote one of the greatest poems in the courtly tradition, and his treatment of courtly conventions is reasonably sustained and consistent. In the *Testament,* however, Henryson's concluding advice that women should not mingle love with false deception, for example, violates all courtly precedent, although it is a fitting moral for a poem which totals the wages of sin in no uncertain way. More generally, we have seen the effect of the poet's orthodox morality on the characterization and plot of the *Testament,* and it is clear that the poem was composed from a recognizably moral point of view. Yet Henryson avails himself of so many courtly details and phrases that the transition between Chaucer's poem and the Scot's sequel on this level is by no means difficult.

Although Henryson was not a court poet and wrote a century after Chaucer, there is no reason to suppose that he was ignorant of the general rules of courtly love, for, when he so desires, as in *Robene and Makyne,* he can summarize them quite fully and correctly. On the other hand, it must not be thought that there were no transitional pieces between Chaucer and Henryson. Perhaps the most outstanding, the *Kingis Quair* of James I, is certainly a courtly poem, but it was composed by a husband to celebrate the courtship of his wife—

---

plaint of the Black Knight, *The Floure of Curtesye, Reson and Sensuallyte, The Assembly of Gods, The Cuckoo and the Nightingale,* and *The Flower and the Leaf.* This is also true of the *PF,* ll. 120 ff. Occasionally, the poet awakes in a forest. Cf. *HF,* ll. 119 ff., *LGW,* prologue, *F,* ll. 209 ff. An exception is the *Kingis Quair,* where the poet mentions the light coming through his window (ed. A. Lawson, p. 39). James I may have been imitating the *BD* also.

a most uncourtly relationship. A similar attitude is found occasionally in the works of Lydgate. Henryson, although he adopts the paraphernalia of courtly love when it happens to accord with the concepts of romantic love, assumes among other things that marriage is the object of courtship, and his point of view characterizes the decline but not the end of a great tradition.

Compared to Chaucer's careful and correct handling of courtly conventions, Henryson's treatment sometimes appears to be consciously cavalier. At the opening of the *Testament,* for example, in the lines following the description of the weather, Henryson writes that he left his private chapel (ll. 22–35):

> For I traistit that Venus, luifis Quene,
> To quhome sum tyme I hecht obedience,
> My faidit hart of lufe scho wald mak grene,
> And thereupon with humbill reverence,
> I thocht to pray hir hie Magnificence;
> Bot for greit cald as than I lattit was,
> And in my Chalmer to the fyre can pas.
>
> Thocht lufe be hait, yit in ane man of age
> It kendillis nocht sa sone as in youtheid,
> Of quhome the blude is flowing in ane rage,
> And in the auld the curage doif and deid,
> Of quhilk the fyre outward is best remeid;
> To help be Phisike quhair that nature faillit
> I am expert, for baith I have assailit.

This combination of frank realism and commonplaces from courtly love is rather startling at first glance: the poet states that he had formerly served Venus, Queen of Love, and that he thought of praying to Her Excellence with humble reverence. He adds, however, that it was too cold to do so. He then remarks that old age makes love difficult of performance, and prescribes a medicine which he has found to be helpful in cases where nature has failed.

Henryson seems to be referring, with some humorous self-disparagement, to his own difficulties with love at an advanced age. His remarks may appear unusual and perhaps unexpected in view of the treatment of the same tradition by his acknowledged master, but this general change in attitude from idealistic to realistic, or even satiric, simply reflects a change in the respective societies of the two poets and documents a stage in the decay of feudalism. For much of the complex ritual of courtly love had apparently fallen of its own irrelevant and unintelligible weight in Henryson's time.[36]

With the *Taill of Schir Chantecleir and the Foxe,* we may perhaps approach a little nearer to Henryson's personal attitude toward courtly love. This fable tells the same story as Chaucer's *Nun's Priest's Tale* but, although there are many minor echoes in Henryson's version, none of them are particularly extensive or noteworthy. An interesting part of the Scot's fable, however, is a disgression on marriage by three of Chantecleir's wives. Between them, the wives run the gamut of courtly, realistic, and orthodox views toward marriage when they learn of the supposed death of their husband and, in the course of the disgression, Henryson's own point of view becomes more ascertainable.

[36] A curious clue to Henryson's lines presents itself in the *Book of the Duchess* (ll. 34–40). Taken literally and not without a touch of humor, Chaucer's remarks indicate that he has been unable to enjoy love for eight years, while Henryson's lines offer robust and complementary comment plus a diagnosis of and prescription for such a condition. In the light of Henryson's thorough and admiring study of "worthie Chaucer glorious," the Scot may conceivably have had Chaucer's lines in mind when he composed the opening lines of the *Testament.* Cf. further, *Confessio Amantis,* ed. G. C. Macaulay, III, 2367 ff.

What Chaucer meant by the lines is a different problem which will probably never be settled. I have suggested elsewhere that Chaucer may be making a conventional, courtly gesture of respect for the Duchess Blanche. Cf. "A Note on Chaucer's Attitude toward Love," *Speculum,* XVII (October, 1942), 570–74. Cf. further, however, Professor R. S. Loomis' scholarly note, "Chaucer's Eight Years' Sickness," *MLN,* LIX (March, 1944), 178–80, where a possible model for the span of eight years is established and any significance beyond the conventional is scouted. Professor Loomis does not discuss why Chaucer suddenly relinquishes his usual attitude of disavowing activity in the affairs of love, nor does his suggestion that the eight-year span is borrowed dispose of the possibility of a conventional, courtly gesture.

At the news of her husband's death, Pertok behaves in what could be called courtly fashion (ll. 495–501):

> "Allace," quod Pertok, makand sair murning,
> With teiris grit attour hir cheikis fell;
> "Yone wes our drowrie, and our dayis darling,
> Our nichtingall, and als our Orloge bell,
> Our walkryfe watche, us for to warne and tell
> Quhen that Aurora with hir curcheis gray,
> Put up hir heid betwix the nicht and day."

She then proceeds conscientiously with the customary "complaint" (ll. 502–8):

> "Quha sall our lemman be? quha sall us leid?
> Quhen we ar sad, quha sall unto us sing?
> With his sweit Bill he wald brek us the breid,
> In all this warld wes thair ane kynder thing?
> In paramouris he wald do us plesing,
> At his power, as nature did him geif.
> Now efter him, allace, how sall we leif?"

Up to this point, Pertok speaks in a courtly manner which would not be out of place, let us say, in the pleasant satire of the *Nun's Priest's Tale*.

Pertok's courtly sadness, however, is rudely interrupted by Sprutok, whose remarks the Wife of Bath would have understood and relished (ll. 509–15):

> . . . "Ceis sister off your sorrow;
> Ye be to mad ffor him sic murning mais:
> We sall ffair weill; I find, Sanct Johne to borrow,
> The prouerb sayis, 'als gude lufe cummis as gais.'
> I will put on my haly dais clais,
> And mak me fresch agane this Jolie may,
> Syne chant this sang, 'wes never wedow sa gay!'"

Nor is Sprutok unaware of the courtly point of view, for she goes into quasi-courtly detail concerning Chantecleir's various inadequacies (ll. 516–22):

"He wes angry and held us ay in aw,
And woundit with the speir off Jelowsy.
Off chalmerglew, Pertok, full weill ye knaw,
Waistit he wes, off Nature cauld and dry;
Sen he is gone, thairfoir, Sister, say I,
Be blyith in baill, ffor that is best remeid:
Let quik to quik, and deid ga to the deid."

It is clear, however, that Sprutok is not at home in the courtly tradition. The Cock's severity and fearsomeness are not faults which are
stressed in courtly love, while the characteristic of jealousy of which
Sprutok complains is an essential virtue in the true courtly lover.
And Sprutok places her main argument on the more realistic grounds
of Chantecleir's lack of "chamber-fun."

Sprutok is a new, different, and, in a sense, transitional characterization. A realist at heart, she has only a nodding acquaintance with
the courtly tradition, but she does not hesitate to adapt any courtly
notions which lie at hand, as long as they appear to support her realistic point of view. It is more than likely that Henryson quite consciously portrayed Sprutok mangling courtly conventions in the
course of his satire on contemporary attitudes.

The courtly Pertok is quickly convinced by the realistic arguments
of Sprutok. In fact, the poet emphasizes her shift of opinion by saying that she spoke with "feinyeit faith befoir." Hence, as the sole
exponent of the courtly attitude, Pertok's easy defection makes both
her and her former views appear insincere and ridiculous (ll. 524–
29):

"In lust but lufe he set all his delyte;
Sister, ye wait, off sic as him ane scoir
Wald not suffice to slaik our appetyte.
I hecht be my hand, sen that he is quyte,
Within ane oulk, ffor schame and I durst speik,
To get ane berne suld better claw oure breik."

This is love on a truly animal level and, in spite of the ironic fact that
this is a beast fable, the sharp contrast is almost shocking and a far

cry, for example, from the light and fanciful tone of the *Nun's Priest's Tale.*

But Toppok has not yet spoken. When she does, the wheel of satire comes almost full circle, for she preaches "lyke ane curate" and presents the rigidly righteous attitude of orthodox morality (ll. 531–43):

> "Yone wes ane verray vengeance from the hevin;
> He wes sa lous, and sa lecherous;
> He had" (quod scho) "kittokis ma than sevin.
> Bot rychteous God, haldand the balandis evin,
> Smytis rycht sair, thocht he be patient,
> For Adulterie, that will thame not repent.

> "Prydefull he wes, and joyit off his sin,
> And comptit not for Goddis favour nor feid,
> Bot traistit ay to rax, and sa to rin,
> Quhill at the last his sinnis can him leid
> To schamefull end, and to yone suddand deid.
> Thairfoir it is the verray hand off God
> That causit him be werryit with the Tod."

According to Toppok's familiar point of view, Chantecleir was punished for his adulterous appetite by the very hand of God.

In his exposition of these three contrasting attitudes toward marriage, Henryson, like Chaucer, does not take sides explicitly—the reader may choose for himself. But it is possible to ascertain Henryson's general attitude, for, unlike Chaucer, the Scot makes little attempt to maintain a consistently neutral point of view. Thus, while the courtly point of view of Pertok is made to appear ridiculous, and Sprutock's realistic views are shown to be brutally animalistic, the orthodox views of Toppok are given the final and most emphatic position in the argument.

As a court poet, Chaucer no doubt had good reason to pretend to impartiality. With Henryson it was unnecessary, and the Scot could throw three conflicting attitudes together for the sake of whatever sparks might fly in the process. Henryson's personal sympathies, one nevertheless suspects, are with Chantecleir, although it is probable that the poet would profess the orthodox views of Toppok if he were seriously challenged. For better or worse, Henryson's morality is that of the twentieth century.

There are minor borrowings from Chaucer in the *Testament of Cresseid*,[37] but the examples already discussed illustrate the relationship of the two poets in general. It is clear that in matters of characterization, plot, and setting, as well as in the less tangible matters of mood and feeling, Henryson was directly and profoundly influenced by Chaucer. The Scot's borrowings are never servile imitations, however, and even his use of conventional devices is characterized by considerable originality. The impression of freshness and creative independence which Henryson's verse conveys is confirmed by a comparison of his work with that of his master.

[37] Some of the details of Cresseid's lament (ll. 416–20) seem to be taken from *LGW* (ll. 1106–11, 1122); Cresseid's swooning (ll. 538–41) imitates a few lines in *Anel* (ll. 169–70, 174–75). Cf. further *Testament*, ll. 113–14 with *SqT*, l. 296 and *Tr*, I, 162–63; and *Testament*, ll. 411, 465, with *Anel*, ll. 242, 197. There are many details in the planet portraits which may come from Chaucer. For Saturn's weapons (ll. 166–67) cf. *Gen Prol* to *CT*, ll. 104–5, 108; for Jupiter's nature cf. *Rom*, ll. 539–44, 548, 562–63, 565–66, 569–70, 573–74, 581; for the armor of Mars (ll. 186–88) cf. *Mars*, ll. 95–101; for the character of Venus (ll. 218–38) cf. *BD*, ll. 617–20, 626–49; and for some of Mercury's characteristics (ll. 246–50), cf. *Gen Prol* to the *CT*, ll. 411, 422, 425–26. Many of these resemblances are discussed in detail in the next chapter.

Chapter V

THE PLANET PORTRAITS

*T*HE DESCRIPTION of the seven planets in the *Testament of Cresseid* is perhaps the most lively and arresting in the whole of English literature. Approximately one third of the poem is devoted to the planets and the trial over which they preside, and they play an essential part in the punishment of Cresseid. The present chapter is an attempt to clear the way for a study of the origins and sources of the planet portraits and thus to shed some light upon the poet's manner of handling his materials.

Before discussing the planets individually, I should like to suggest that Henryson is indebted to Lydgate's *Assembly of Gods* for many of the details in his treatment of the trial of Cresseid before a parliament of planets.[1] Although a few scholars have concluded that Henryson probably knew the works of Lydgate in general and his *Fables* in particular,[2] no one has noticed the Scot's debt to the English poet in the *Testament of Cresseid.*[3] For the *Assembly of Gods* and the

[1] The *Assembly of Gods* has not found an unquestioned place in the Lydgate canon. Cf. H. N. MacCracken, ed., *The Minor Poems of John Lydgate,* I, xxxv–xxxvi. Cf. further, however, O. L. Triggs, ed., *The Assembly of Gods,* pp. xi–xii. The text of Triggs is used throughout.

[2] H. N. MacCracken feels that Lydgate's influence may be found in Henryson's prologue to the *Fables* and six minor poems, and concludes that "it is probable that Henryson knew Lydgate's verses." *Studies in the Life and Writings of John Lydgate,* p. 413. Gregory Smith compares the two versions of Aesop's *Fables* and states that "Henryson was familiar with Lydgate's *Aesop.*" *Poems of . . . Henryson,* I, xxxix. Cf. further, A. R. Diebler, *Henrisone's Fabeldichtungen, passim,* where minor verbal parallels are perhaps overstressed, and M. Plessow, *Geschichte der Fabeldichtung in England bis zu John Gay,* pp. xlv ff.

[3] Gregory Smith's suggestion that Henryson's portrait of Saturn owes something to Lydgate's portrait in the *Assembly* is an exception to this statement. *Poems of . . . Henryson,* I, xxxix.

Testament of Cresseid describe a court of the gods in which a "parliament"[4] judges a "trespass"[5] or "despite"[6] in order to deliver a "sentence."[7] In the *Assembly*, Eolus has stirred up the elements on land and sea and incurred the displeasure of Diana and Neptune; in the *Testament*, Cresseid has blasphemed her gods and incurred the displeasure of Cupid and Venus.

The plaintiffs in both poems make similar points. First, their reputations have been injured: in the *Assembly*, Neptune objects to the "hurt of my name" (l. 98), while Diana declares "among the pepyll lost ys my name" (l. 132); in the *Testament*, Cupid dwells upon the "sclander and defame Injurious" (l. 284) caused by Cresseid. Secondly, the plaintiffs assert that an injury to one god is an injury to all the gods: in the *Assembly*, Diana states that the injury is "to all the goddes an hygh dyspleser" (l. 73); in the *Testament*, Cupid asserts that anyone who injures one god "to all Goddis he dois baith lak and schame" (l. 276). Thirdly, the plaintiffs claim that a specially protected person or group of persons has been injured: in the *Assembly*, Neptune declares that damage has been done to those "to whom I promysyd, bothe in good and yll, To be her protectour in aduersyte" (ll. 122–23); in the *Testament*, Cupid states that an injury has been received by Venus "to quhome I schew my grace abone all uther" (l. 287). Lastly, the plaintiffs then demand punishment and revenge: in the *Assembly*, Diana says, "Execute your fury vppon Eolus" (l. 53) and "let hym be punysshyd aftyr hys offence" (l. 76), while Neptune adds, "Let hym nat escape out of your daungere, Tyll he haue made full seethe and recompence" (ll. 96–97); in the *Testament*, Cupid declares, "Me think with pane we suld mak recompence . . . Thairfoir ga help to revenge I yow pray" (ll. 291, 294). The parallel is detailed and extensive.

[4] *Assembly*, l. 26; *Testament*, l. 266. References to Henryson's text are taken from H. H. Wood, ed., *The Poems and Fables of Robert Henryson*.

[5] *Assembly*, l. 221; *Testament*, l. 371.   [6] *Assembly*, l. 121; *Testament*, l. 304.

[7] *Assembly*, l. 136; *Testament*, l. 151.

At the trial, two judges are prominent in each poem. In the *Assembly,* Minos and Pluto are to decide the fate of Eolus; in the *Testament,* Saturn and Cynthia decide the fate of Cresseid. Further, a selection of judges with the consent of the plaintiffs takes place in both poems. In the *Assembly,* Neptune accepts Phebe in the following manner: "'I shall abyde,' quod he, 'her ordynaunce'" (l. 245). In the *Testament,* Cupid accepts Saturn and Cynthia with a similar phrase: "'I am content' (quod he), 'to tak thay twa'" (l. 301). Again, the judges in both poems spend some time deliberating before coming to a verdict. In the *Assembly,* "And, when the god Pluto awhyle had hym bethought, He rownyed with Mynos to know what was to do" (ll. 141–42); in the *Testament,* "Than thus proceidit Saturne and the Mone, Quhen thay the mater rypelie had degest" (ll. 302–3). The resemblance between the two poems ceases here, for the trial is interrupted in the *Assembly of Gods* and no decision is reached.

It is possible that Henryson borrowed words, phrases, and details of procedure for his trial scene from the *Assembly of Gods.* If such is the case, the Scot's use of the material makes an excellent study of the poet at work, for the earlier poem is an admittedly poor performance,[8] and its description of the parliament of the gods is almost as long as the entire *Testament.* The operative details of the involved complaint of the plaintiffs, the judicial manner of the judges, and the legal niceties of selecting an arbiter, which are presented diffusely and at great length in the *Assembly of Gods,* may be found in the *Testament of Cresseid,* but they are carefully subordinated and properly unobtrusive. Henryson selected his material with a sure touch and presented it in a condensed and effective form.

Turning to the planet portraits, we may note that by substituting astrological qualities for the mythological qualities of the ancient gods, Chaucer had pioneered and made poetic capital of the astro-

[8] Cf. O. L. Triggs, ed., *The Assembly of Gods,* p. xli.

logical magic in which his age had come to believe.[9] Writing nearly a century later, Henryson took full advantage of this fact. The *Testament of Cresseid* contains many elements of astrology. In the opening lines, the poet dates the poem by means of an astronomical periphrase in which he describes the Sun and Venus in opposition, a combination which signifies, as Lilly says, "A barren time . . . the Native impudent and bold in his wantonnesse and Lust, wholly occupied in scurvy and sordid actions, whereby he incurres great Infamy, Scandall and Disgrace," [10] and which sets the tone for the burden of the poem. The planets are ranked according to their astrological order, and Mercury is chosen speaker, a choice which accords with his influence over logic and debate.[11] The choice of Saturn and Cynthia to deliver the verdict of leprosy is fitting, according to the astrological qualities of the humors, and the poet's treatment of the disease shows a detailed knowledge of astrological medicine.[12]

It is not surprising, therefore, to find that Henryson's planet portraits are fundamentally astrological in character, although they are supplemented by details from many sources. At their first appearance, the planets are described as (ll. 147–50),

> The seven Planetis discending fra thair Spheiris,
> Quhilk hes power of all thing generabill
> To reull and steir be thair greit Influence,
> Wedder and wind, and coursis variabill.

These are the general astrological qualities associated with the planets; the more specific qualities appear in the individual portraits.

I

The first to be described is Saturn (ll. 151–68):

[9] Cf. T. O. Wedel, *The Mediaeval Attitude toward Astrology*, pp. 142–44; J. S. P. Tatlock, "Astrology and Magic in the *Franklin's Tale*," *Anniversary Papers . . . Kittredge*, pp. 339–40; W. C. Curry, *Chaucer and the Mediaeval Sciences*, pp. 119–20.
[10] W. Lilly, *Christian Astrology*, p. 684.   [11] *Ibid.*, pp. 77–78.
[12] Cf. *supra*, pp. 42–46.

And first of all Saturne gave his sentence,
Quhilk gave to Cupide litill reverence,
Bot, as ane busteous Churle on his maneir,
Come crabitlie with auster luik and cheir.

.   .   .   .   .

His face [fronsit], his lyre was lyke the Leid,
His teith chatterit, and cheverit with the Chin,
His Ene drowpit, how sonkin in his heid,
Out of his Nois the Meldrop fast can rin,
With lippis bla and cheikis leine and thin;
The Iceschoklis that fra his hair doun hang
Was wonder greit, and as ane speir als lang.

Atouir his belt his lyart lokkis lay
Felterit unfair, ouirfret with Froistis hoir,
His garmound and his gyis full gay of gray,
His widderit weid fra him the wind out woir;
Ane busteous bow within his hand he boir,
Under his girdill ane flasche of felloun flanis,
Fedderit with Ice, and heidit with hailstanis.

Elsewhere in the *Testament,* Henryson refers to Saturn as the highest
of the planets (l. 297), and as "cruell Saturne! fraward and angrie,"
imploring him to be "gracious as thou was never" in dealing with
Cresseid (ll. 323, 327-28); he also speaks of Saturn's "wraikfull sentence" as a doom which is "to malitious" (ll. 329, 324).

The nature of Henryson's characterization of Saturn may perhaps
be best revealed by a comparison with Lilly's summary of the astrological qualities of the planet:

He is the supreamest or highest of all the Planets; is placed betwixt *Jupiter*
and the Firmanent, he is not very bright or glorious, or doth he twinckle or
sparkle, but is of a Pale, Wan or Leaden, Ashy colour . . . He is a Diur-
nall Planet, Cold and Dry (being farre removed from the heat of the Sun)
and moyst Vapours, Melancholick, Earthly, Masculine, the greater Infor-
tune, author of Solitarinesse, Malevolent, &c. Then he is profound in
Imagination, in his Acts severe, . . . in all manner of actions austere.

Then he is envious, covetous, jealous and mistrustfull, timorus, sordid, outwardly dissembling, sluggish, suspitious, stubborne, a contemner of women, a close lyar, malicious, murmuring, never contented, ever repining. Most part his Body more cold and dry, of a middle stature; his Complexion pale, swartish or muddy, his Eyes little and black, looking downward, a broad Forehead, black or sad Haire, and it hard or rugged, great Eares; hanging lowring Eye-browes, thick Lips and Nose, . . . his Knees and Feet indecent, many times shoveling or hitting one against another &c. . . In generall he signifieth Husbandmen, Clownes, Beggars, Day-labourers, Old men, Fathers, Grandfathers, . . . all quartan Agues proceeding of cold, dry and melancholly Distempers, Leprosies, Rheumes, Consumptions, black Jaundies, Palsies, Tremblings . . . He ruleth over Lead . . . He causeth Cloudy, Darke, obscure Ayre, cold and hurtfull . . . He delighteth in the East quarter of Heaven, and causeth Easterne Winds . . . As to age, he relates to decreped old men . . . his enemies Mars and Venus.[13]

Similar but less extensive descriptions of Saturn may be found in many astrological works of the Middle Ages.[14]

It is evident that Henryson's Saturn is fundamentally a dramatization of astrological detail. In general, a cruel, perverse, angry Saturn, who comes crabbedly with austere look and face to impose a vengeful sentence which is too malicious, is a characterization that conforms literally to Lilly's adjectives "Masculine," "Malevolent," "austere," "mistrustfull," "suspitious," "stubborne," "malicious," "murmuring," and so on. More particularly, Henryson, like Lilly, calls Saturn the

[13] W. Lilly, op. cit., pp. 57–61. Although Lilly wrote more than a century after Henryson's day, the astrologer offers a convenient and typical summary of astrological lore current in the poet's times.

[14] For a discussion of pertinent astrological works translated into Latin during the twelfth century, cf. Wedel, op. cit., pp. 4 ff., 49 ff. The Arabian astrologers offer the most extensive descriptions of the planets. Thus, Albohazen in his Liber de Fatis Astrorum gives a description of Saturn similar to Lilly's (sig. a₃ verso); Alchabitus in his Libellus Ysagogicus emphasizes Saturn's connection with melancholy and leprosy, his dark garments, and his downcast eyes (sig. bb₅, recto and verso). The description of Saturn in Ptolemy's Quadripartitum is too brief to be pertinent. Cf. N. Pruckner, ed., Ptolemaei . . . Quadripartitum, pp. 6, 30, 55. The essentials of the astrological description appear also in the encyclopedists. Cf. Bartholomaeus Anglicus, De Proprietatibus Rerum, tr. Trevisa, Bk. VIII, chap. xxiii.

highest of the planets, and Saturn's lack of reverence for Cupid is in character, because of the further fact that Cupid is the son of Saturn's enemy, Venus. As a "busteous Churle," Saturn fits Lilly's group of day-laborers; the "lyre . . . lyke lead" repeats Saturn's leaden color; the "Ene drowpit" parallels Lilly's statement that the eyes look downward; Henryson's statement that Saturn "come crabitlie" echoes Lilly's description of the planet's awkward gait; the "teith chatterit, and cheverit with the Chin" suggests Lilly's mention of palsy; the "Meldrop" running from the nose suggests rheum. Henryson's Saturn is truly a "contemner of women." I have commented elsewhere upon the accuracy of the poet's treatment of the planet's cold, dry qualities and melancholic temperament in regard to Cresseid's leprosy.[15]

A few possible sources of minor detail may be mentioned. Lydgate describes Saturn in *The Assembly of Gods* (ll. 281–87):

> But he was clad me thought straungely,
> For of frost & snow was all his aray;
> In hys hand he helde a fawchon all blody.
> Hyt semyd by his chere as he wold make a fray.
> A bawdryk of isykles about hys nek gay
> He had, and aboue an hygh on hys hede,
> Cowchyd *with* hayle stonys, he weryd a crowne of leede.[16]

The only literal parallels to the *Testament* are the words "isykles" and "hayle stonys," yet the treatment is similar, and these lines are perhaps Henryson's most obvious source for his unusual emphasis upon Saturn's coldness.[17]

---

[15] Cf. *supra*, pp. 44–47.

[16] O. L. Triggs, ed., *The Assembly of Gods*, ll. 281–87. The authorship of this poem has been queried. Cf. H. N. MacCracken, ed., *The Minor Poems of . . . Lydgate*, I, xxxv–xxxvi.

[17] The iconology of Saturn is instructive. In classical art he is depicted as mournful but dignified, with a veil over his head and a sickle in his hand. In the mythological illustrations of the Middle Ages, often evolved entirely from texts, Saturn wears a veil, carries a sickle and a scythe, and holds a dragon biting its tail. The process of castration and the act of devouring a child is often found. The astrological representations,

A few lines from Chaucer's description of the yeoman in the prologue to the *Canterbury Tales* may account for some of the weapons
with which Henryson equips Saturn. Chaucer had written (ll. 104–
5, 108):

> A sheef of pecock arwes, bright and kene,
> Under his belt he bar ful thriftily,
>
> .   .   .   .   .
>
> And in his hand he baar a myghty bowe.

Henryson duplicates the references to the sheaf of arrows under the
belt and a mighty bow borne in the hand (ll. 166–67).

II

Henryson presents the following portrait of Jupiter (ll. 169–82):

> Than Juppiter, richt fair and amiabill,
> God of the Starnis in the Firmament,
> And Nureis to all thing generabill,
> Fra his Father Saturne far different,
> With burelie face, and browis bricht and brent,
> Upon his heid ane Garland, wonder gay,
> Of flouris fair, as it had bene in May.
>
> His voice was cleir, as Cristall wer his Ene,
> As goldin wyre sa glitterand was his hair;
> His garmound and his gyis full [gay] of grene,
> With golden listis gilt on everie gair;
> Ane burlie brand about his midill bair;
> In his richt hand he had ane groundin speir,
> Of his Father the wraith fra us to weir.

into which the mythological merged in the late Middle Ages, depicted Saturn with a
mattock or spade, and later a staff or crutch, resulting eventually in a cripple with a
wooden leg. Cf. E. Panofsky, *Studies in Iconology*, pp. 76 ff. The lack of influence
of such illustrations upon Henryson is evident. On the other hand, if the Scot's portrait was influenced by any personification of Winter, it has not been found. Cf.
R. Steele, ed., *Lydgate and Burgh's Secrees of Old Philisoffres*, pp. 46–47, and Bartholomaeus Anglicus, *op. cit.*, Bk. IX, chap. viii, for typical examples. Cf. further R. Tuve,
Seasons and Months, pp. 122 ff. The personification of Father Time or Death is closer,
but Henryson's portrait cannot be said to owe anything to these sources.

This characterization seems to have evolved from a blending of the astrological qualities of Jupiter with elements of the dream-allegory.

The poet's debt to astrology may be indicated by the description of this planet in Albohazen:

Iuppiter est planeta equalitatis: communitatis: melioramenti: intellectus: sensus: & pietatis . . . significat bonitatem: meliorationem: legem simplicitatem . . . Abhorret saturnum & eius naturas: prohibet & retrahit eum a suis malis operibus. Est formose apparentie & composite persone: mansuetus: fidelis: legalis: & pietosus: precipit & ostendit bonitatem: prohibet & abhorret malu[m] . . . per eum clarificatur aer: currunt venti & . . . pluuie . . . Et per sui demonstrationem & fortitudinem in nono mense a conceptione creature liberatur natus: & exit ad mundum & ad eius quietem: & ad aerem: & ab angustia ventris & suis tenebris liberatur . . . creatus & factus est iuppiter de claritate aeris et lumine suo: ac de vento eius limpido et purgato.[18]

Phrases such as Albohazen's "planeta equalitatis . . . Est formose apparentie & composite persone: mansuetus" establish the similarity to Henryson's "richt fair and amiabill" planet; the statement that "per eum clarificatur aer: currunt venti & . . . pluuie" emphasizes the connection with the elements which is found in the *Testament;* the remark that "per sui demonstrationem & fortitudinem in nono mense a conceptione creature liberatur natus" parallels the poet's assertion that Jupiter is a nurse to all created things; and the Arabian astrologer's "Abhorret saturnum & eius naturas: prohibet & retrahit eum a suis malis operibus" suggests Henryson's reference to Jupiter as far different from his father, Saturn, from whose wrath he shields us.[19]

---

[18] *Op. cit.,* sig. a₄, *recto.* Cf. also Alchabitus, *op. cit.,* sig. bb₆, *recto,* and Albumasar, *Introductorium in Astronomiam,* sig. h₄, *recto.* Ptolemy gives a less extensive description, but cf. Lilly, *op. cit.,* pp. 61–65.

[19] Many elements of common mythology may be found in the portrait of Jupiter (and the other portraits), although the emphasis is elsewhere. Astrology and mythology overlapped to some extent. The mythographers, however, stress the fact that Jupiter overthrew his father, a detail that is not mentioned by the astrologers or Henryson. Jupiter is frequently described as the ruler of all the gods in mythology. Cf. *Thebaid,*

With the more ornamental details of Jupiter's appearance, Henryson leaves the astrological tradition for the dream-allegory. The nature of the poet's borrowing may be illustrated by the description of Idleness in Chaucer's *Romaunt of the Rose* (ll. 539-44, 548, 562-63, 565-66, 569-70, 573-74, 581):

> Hir heer was as yelowe of hewe
> As ony basyn scoured newe;
> Hir flesh [as] tendre as is a chike,
> With bente browis smothe and slyke;
> And by mesure large were
> The openyng of hir yen clere
>
> . . . . .
>
> Hir face whit and wel coloured
>
> . . . . .
>
> And of fyn orfrays hadde she eke
> A chapelet
>
> . . . . .
>
> And faire above that chapelet
> A rose gerland had she sett
>
> . . . . .
>
> Hir heed was tressed queyntely;
> Hir sleves sewid fetisly
>
> . . . . .
>
> And she hadde on a cote of grene
> Of cloth of Gaunt; withouten wene
>
> . . . . .
>
> She ladde a lusty lyf in May.[20]

Henryson duplicates, more or less literally, the well-colored face, the smooth brows, the garland of flowers on the head, the clear eyes, the

---

I, 197–210; *Met.*, I, 177–80; *Argonautica,* I, 690–92; Albricus Philosophus, *De Deorum Imaginibus Libellus,* in A. van Staveren, ed., *Auctores Mythographi Latini,* p. 897; and Myth. Vat. III, in G. H. Bode, ed., *Scriptores Rerum Mythicarum,* pp. 160–65. Such a concept could not fit astrology. But the enmity between Jupiter and Saturn is a commonplace in both traditions. A derivative characterization occurs in medieval iconology where Jupiter is depicted as a judge. Cf. Panofsky, *op. cit.,* pp. 21, 26.

[20] F. N. Robinson, ed., *The Complete Works of Geoffrey Chaucer,* pp. 669–70.

yellow hair, the green garment, and the month of May, although it should be added that these details are quite conventional.[21]

The combination of an astrological characterization with outward details from a personification in dream-allegory is a happy one in this instance, for the astrological Jupiter is amiable and well-favored and the description of Idleness forms a suitable extension of these qualities.

III

The third planet that Henryson describes is Mars (ll. 183–96):

> Nixt efter him come Mars, the God of Ire,
> Of strife, debait, and all dissensioun,
> To chide and fecht, als feirs as ony fyre;
> In hard Harnes, hewmound and Habirgeoun,
> And on his hanche ane roustie fell Fachioun;
> And in his hand he had ane roustie sword;
> Wrything his face with mony angrie word,
>
> Schaikand his sword, befoir Cupide he come
> With reid visage, and grislie glowrand Ene;
> And at his mouth ane bullar stude of fome
> Lyke to ane Bair quhetting his Tuskis kene,
> Richt Tui[t]lyeour lyke, but temperance in tene;
> Ane horne he blew, with mony bosteous brag,
> Quhilk all this warld with weir hes maid to wag.

This portrait is based upon the astrological conception of Mars, with the addition of details which may have been taken from Ovid and Chaucer.

A passage from Albohazen will illustrate the astrological content in the poet's description:

Mars est planeta calidus & siccus: igneus: feruens: nocturnus: femininus: destructor: iratus: victoriosus: diligit occidere & interfectiones: rixas: liti-

---

[21] For comment on Lydgate's frequent use of the comparison of hair to gold wire, cf. J. Schick, ed., *Lydgate's Temple of Glas,* pp. cxxxii, 88–91. For a similar description of Jupiter, suggested by Parr, cf. A. Lawson, ed., *The Kingis Quair,* stanza 1.

gia: & contrariari alteri leuiter infortunat: stultus: non patiens: cito irascitur ira forti: totum cor suum exponit in rebus suis agendis: non ita percipit
cu[m] est iratus: nec manuum retrahit de faciendo id quod incipit:
guerras & facta mouet: prelia facit: & destruit populationes.[22]

Albohazen's "rixas: litigia: & contrariari alteri" is echoed by Henryson's "Of strife, debait, and all dissensioun"; the "non patiens: cito
irascitur ira forti," and the "non ita percipit cu[m] est iratus" suggest the poet's "Richt Tui[t]lyeour lyke, but temperance in tene";
and there are shorter parallels between "igneus" and "fyre," "iratus"
and "Ire," "guerras" and "fecht," and "prelia" and "strife." These are
the typical characteristics of Mars in astrological works.[23]

The poet also describes Mars with stout armor, a helmet, a coat of
mail, a mighty bronze blade on the hip, and a bronze sword in his
hand. Although Mars is generally described with a variety of weapons,[24] the planet's armor in the present case may have been borrowed
in part from Chaucer's *Complaint of Mars*. Describing the god of
war surprised by Phoebus, Chaucer writes (ll. 95–101):

> . . . from his eyen tweyne
> The firi sparkes brosten out for peyne;

---

[22] *Op. cit.*, sig. a₄, *verso*.

[23] In his *Matheseos*, Julius Firmicus Maternus describes Mars as "iracundus . . .
pugna, caedes . . . maledicos . . . inuerecundum . . . controversia." Cf. Pruckner,
ed., *Ptolemaei . . . Quadripartitum*, pp. 22–23. (The authenticity of this passage has
been questioned. Cf. W. Kroll and F. Skutsch, *Iulii Firmici Materni Matheseos*, II,
xiv ff.) In his *Quadripartitum*, Ptolemy refers to Mars as "iracundus . . . primus in
bello, uilipendet omnia . . . superbus." Pruckner, ed., *Ptolemaei . . . Quadripartitum*, p. 57. Alchabitus deals briefly with Mars, but Albumasar repeats the customary
details at length (*op. cit.*, sig. h₄) such as "ira, controversus, dissentiones, litigia, pugna,
atrox, maledicus, multi murmuri." Cf. further Lilly, *op. cit.*, pp. 65–68.

[24] In classical mythology, Mars is described with a shield, spear, helmet, lance, and
sword, among other weapons. Cf. *Aeneid*, VIII, 700–701; *Met.*, XIV, 806–7. Mars
also has a chariot. Cf. *Aeneid*, XII, 331–36. The mythographers stressed the Venus-
Vulcan episode to the exclusion of almost everything else. Cf. B. Bunte, ed., *Hygini Astronomica*, p. 79, and the *Mythologicon* of Fulgentius, in A. van Staveren, ed., *Auctores Mythographi Latini*, pp. 682–83. Nor do the encyclopedists stress the weapons
of Mars. Cf. Bartholomaeus Anglicus, *op. cit.*, Bk. VIII, chap. xxv. Cf. further, Panofsky,
op. cit., pp. 49, 56, 162 ff. Accordingly, it seems that Henryson's source is closer to
classical mythology, although he does not mention the spear, lance, or chariot,

And hente his hauberk, that ley hym besyde.
Fle wolde he not, ne myghte himselven hide.

He throweth on his helm of huge wyghte,
And girt him with his swerd, and in his hond
His myghty spere, as he was wont to fyghte . . .[25]

Henryson duplicates Chaucer's "Hauberk," "helm," and "swerd" (in fact, the Scot equips Mars with two swords, perhaps because of the exigencies of the rime). Henryson's "Harnes" is a generic term which could apply to several of the weapons Chaucer specifies.

The lines in which the poet likens Mars to a boar have no precedent in the usual descriptions of that god or planet. In the *Metamorphoses,* however, Ovid describes a boar in a similar manner (VIII, 284–85, 287–89, 369) :

Sanguine et igne micant oculi, riget ardua cervix,
et setae similes rigidis hastilibus horrent:

. . . . .

fervida cum rauco latos stridore per armos
spuma fluit, dentes aequantur dentibus Indis,
fulmen ab ore venit, frondes afflatibus ardent.

. . . . .

Dentibus ille ferox in querno stipite tritis.

Ovid's "sanguine et igne micant oculi" suggests Henryson's "grislie glowrand Ene"; Ovid's "spuma," the Scot's "fome"; and the "dentibus ille ferox in querno stipite tritis," the "Bair quhetting his Tuskis kene." There are other descriptions of boars in literature preceding Henryson, but none has been discovered which resembles the poet's so closely.[26]

Although there are many details in Henryson's portrait of Mars

---

[25] Professor Robinson's statement that Chaucer's description of Mars is astrological seems doubtful; the armament, for example, appears to be entirely mythological. Cf. Robinson, ed., *Works of . . . Chaucer,* p. 973, note to l. 97.

[26] Most of the boar similes in literature appear to be derived from Ovid. Cf. *Thebaid,* XI, 530–33. The *Ovide Moralisé* contains an expanded version of Ovid which bears no closer resemblance to Henryson. Cf. C. de Boer, ed., *Ovide Moralisé, Koninklijke Akademie,* III, 157 ff. Cf. further Gower's *Vox Clamantis,* in G. C. Macaulay, ed.,

(and his portraits of the other planets) which cannot be traced,[27] we are able to note the primary source and observe how the poet goes about creating his characterizations, assembling concrete details from a variety of sources to embellish an astrological conception.[28]

IV

The poet gives a lengthy portrait of the Sun (ll. 197–217):

> Than fair Phebus, Lanterne & Lamp of licht
> Of man and beist, baith frute and flourishing,
> Tender Nureis, and banischer of nicht,
> And of the warld causing, be his moving
> And Influence, lyfe in all eirdlie thing,
> Without comfort of quhome, of force to nocht
> Must all ga die that in this warld is wrocht.

> As King Royall he raid upon his Chair
> The quhilk Phaeton gydit sum tyme upricht;
> The brichtnes of his face quhen it was bair
> Nane micht behald for peirsing of his sicht.
> This goldin Cart with fyrie bemis bricht
> Four yokkit steidis full different of hew,
> But bait or tyring, throw the Spheiris drew.

> The first was soyr, with Mane als reid as Rois,
> Callit Eoye into the Orient;
> The secund steid to Name hecht Ethios,
> Quhitlie and paill, and sum deill ascendent;

Works of John Gower, IV, 31. Chaucer uses a boar simile (*KnT*, ll. 1658–59). Cf. also J. R. R. Tolkien and E. V. Gordon, eds., *Gawain and the Green Knight*, pp. 48–49.

[27] No precedent, for example, has been found for the horn which Mars blows. There may be some connection, however, with Mars and the conventional description of the month of March: the weapons ascribed to March are similar and this month is depicted occasionally as a warrior blowing a horn. Cf. J. C. Webster, *The Labors of the Months*, pp. 138 ff. and plates cited.

[28] For generally similar descriptions of Mars by Lydgate, suggested by Parr, cf. H. Bergen, ed., *Lydgate's Troy Book*, prologue, 1–21; A. Erdmann, ed., *Lydgate's Siege of Thebes*, EETS, ll. 2553–67, 4690–97; O. L. Triggs, ed., *The Assembly of Gods*, ll. 260–66.

The thrid Peros, richt hait and richt fervent;
The feird was blak, callit Philologie
Quhilk rollis Phebus doun into the sey.

The first stanza, which describes the Sun's nature, appears to be derived from astrology; the second and third stanzas, which are devoted to a description of the Sun's chariot and horses, contain material from mythology.

The astrological nature of Henryson's first stanza may be indicated by a passage from Albohazen: [29]

Sol est lumen & candela c[o]eli gubernator mundi: factor temporum . . . per eum mouetur omnis res se mouens: per eum nascitur omnis res nascens: crescit omnis res crescens: crescit omne folium & maturatur omnis fructus. Ipse est spiritus c[o]eli magnus. Cum eo vivificantur signa[.] Et quodlibet signum quando est in eo habet maioritatem super alia signa: quam ipsum viuificat & illuminat & dat ei fortitudinem & calorem & applicat calorem: fortitudinem & virtutem illius signi terre: quia natura & facta sua apparent in omnibus rebus & cunctis animatis & in animatis existentibus in terra . . . Per solum fit decursus aquarum: motus ventorum. Per eum nascuntur nubes & veniunt pluuie . . . & lux & lumen illud vadunt crescendo sicut crescit creatura . . . et transmittit eius subtile ad summitatem arborum & ramorum: & quelibet arbor & omnis planta & herba recipiunt suam partem de eo . . . quis natura sua operatur in omnibus naturis & nulla naturarum aliarum operatur in eo.

Albohazen's "lumen & candela c[o]eli," combined with his "lux & lumen," furnish a model for Henryson's "Phebus, Lanterne & Lamp of licht"; the astrologer's phrases "crescit creatura" and "crescit omnis res crescens: crescit omne folium & maturatur omnis fructus" suggest the Scot's "Phebus . . . Of man and beist, baith frute and flourisching, Tender Nureis, and banischer of nicht"; and Albohazen's "per eum mouetur omnis res se movens: per eum nascitur omnis res nascens," as well as his "quia natura & facta sua apparent in omnibus rebus & cunctis animatis & in animatis existentibus in terra," forms a

[29] *Op. cit.*, sig. a₂, *verso.*

parallel to the poet's phrase "And of the warld causing be his moving And Influence, lyfe in all eirdlie thing." Henryson's concluding remark that without the comfort of Phoebus everything in this world must necessarily die is implicit in Albohazen's entire treatment.[30]

Henryson's second stanza, describing the Sun riding in his horse-drawn chariot which Phaeton once guided wrongly, appears to be derived from the *Metamorphoses* (II, 19 ff.) where Ovid tells the story in detail, referring to the brightness of the Sun's face which none may behold without loss of sight (II, 21–23), to the Sun's chariot (II, 107–10), and to the four horses (II, 153–55).

The poet's third stanza, which names and describes the four horses of the Sun, poses an interesting problem. Henryson's editors, although they agree that the names of the horses derive from Ovid, disagree specifically over the spelling of the fourth horse's name, *Philologie.* The first mention of the question occurs in Skeat, who adopts the spelling, *Philegoney,* remarking:

The names of the four horses are curiously corrupted from the names given in Ovid, *Met.* ii, 153, viz. Eöus, Aethon, Pyröeis, and Phlegon. As *Eous* means "belonging to the dawn," we may consider the words *into the Orient,* i.e. in the East, as explanatory of the name *Eoy;* "called Eoy, (which signifies) in the East." As to the name of the last horse, it was obviously meant to take the form Philegoney, in order to rime with *sey* (sea), and I have therefore restored this form. The two authorities . . . give it in

---

[30] The concept of the Sun as the source of light is, of course, a commonplace, but the concept of the Sun as a creator is not so common. Cf. *De Divinis Nominibus* by Pseudo-Dionysius, in J. P. Migne, ed., *Patrologia Latina,* CXXII, 1131, where the Sun is described as "ad generationem sensibilium corporum comittitur, et ad vitam ea movet." Cf. further Cicero, *De re publica,* VI, xvii; Pliny, *Naturalis historia,* II, 4; Ausonius, *Ecl,* VII, 4 ff. The concept of the Sun as a tender nurse is more rare. In *De re publica,* Cicero calls the Sun "mens mundi et temperatio" (VI, xvii); and Pseudo-Dionysius says the Sun "nutrit, et auget, et perficit, et purgat, et renovat." *Ibid.* Cf. further Bartholomaeus Anglicus, *op. cit.,* Bk. VIII, chap. xxviii, and H. Bergen, ed., *Lydgate's Troy Book,* II, 5591–93. As a whole, these concepts are scattered, incomplete, and mainly mythological. The astrologers present a more extensive and pertinent description. Cf. the *Matheseos* of Firmicus, in Pruckner's edition, p. 23 and Albumasar, *op. cit.,* sig. h_5.

the amazing form *Philologie (Philologee)*, which can only mean "philology!" [31]

G. G. Smith prefers the spelling *Phlegonie*, and comments:

The names of the four steeds of the Sun are drawn, with some latitude in spelling, from Ovid, *Met.*, ii, 153–155:—

"Interea volucres Pyroeis, et Eous, et Aethon,
Solis equi, quartusque Phlegon, hinnitibus auras
Flammiferis implent, pedibusque repagula pulsant."

The last (Phlegon) appears in both texts in the quaint form *Philologie* or *Philologee*. Skeat reconstructs the line—

"The feird was blak callit Philegoney;"

but it seems better to read thus—

"The feird was blak [and] callit Phlegonie." [32]

H. H. Wood returns to one of the two original spellings, *Philologie*, apparently under a misconception, and comments:

The names of the four steeds derive from Ovid's *Metamorphoses* . . . In both *Charteris* and *Thynne*, *Phlegon* appears as *Philologee*. K and SJ give the correct reading. [33]

Bruce Dickins adopts Skeat's spelling and remarks:

Philegoney, Phlegon (Ovid, Met. II, 154), an obvious correction of the Charteris *Philologie* and Thynne's *Philologee*. [34]

Apparently Henryson's editors were unaware of the fact that the various traditions of the Sun's horses, long established in Greek literature, [35] may be found to resolve themselves into two main streams in the Middle Ages. For lack of precedent, I have arbitrarily labeled them the Ovidian and the Fulgentian. Modern scholarship, it may be noted, has in general erred in emphasizing the former and

---

[31] W. W. Skeat, ed., *Chaucerian and Other Pieces*, p. 523.

[32] G. G. Smith, *The Poems of Robert Henryson*, I, 48.

[33] H. H. Wood, *The Poems and Fables of Robert Henryson*, p. 256. K and SJ are late texts.

[34] B. Dickins, ed., *The Testament*, p. 38.

[35] Cf. W. H. Roscher, *Lexicon* (Leipzig, 1884–1937), *s.v. Helios* and *Phaeton*.

ignoring the latter.[36] The traditions vary in presenting different names for the four horses and a different set of individual characteristics for each horse. Since Ovid, alone, does not give individual characteristics for each horse, although his followers do, I am illustrating the Ovidian tradition by the *Ovide Moralisé*. In this work, the Sun's horses are described thus (II, 292–96):

> Pirouz, qui rouges a le poil
> A droite samblance de fu
> Et Eoüz, qui blanc refu,
> Ethon, cui resplent la colour,
> Et Phlegon, plains de grant chalour.[37]

This version is followed consistently by Berchorius,[38] Froissart,[39] and in part, by Lydgate[40] and Chaucer.[41]

On the other hand, Fulgentius writes of the same four horses as follows:

Unde & ipsius equis condigna sic nomina posuerunt, id est Erythreus, Actaeon, Lampos, Philogeus. Erythreus Graece rubeus dicitur, quod a matutino Sol lumine rubicundus exsurgat: Actaeon splendens dicitur, quod tertiae horae [momentis] vehemens insistens lucidior fulgeat: Lampos vero ardens, dum ad umbilicum diei centratum conscenderit circulum. Philogeus Graece terram amans dicitur, quod hora nona proclivior, vergens occasibus pronus incumbat.[42]

This Fulgentian version is followed by the three Vatican mythographers[43] and Gower.[44] In order to bring out the differences and, at

---

[36] "Ovids glänzende Darstellung der Sage ist fast für alle späteren Dichter massgebend gewesen . . . Auch die mythographische Litteratur ist fast ganz durch Ovid beeinflusst." Roscher, *op. cit., s.v. Phaeton.*

[37] Ed. de Boer, *Koninklijke Akademie*, Vol. XXX, No. 3.

[38] *Opera Omnia*, I, 400.

[39] *La Prison Amoureuse*, I, 272, in M. A. Scheler, ed., *Oeuvres de Froissart.*

[40] H. Bergen, ed., *Troy Book*, I, 623, 626–29; II, 2386–87; III, 9–10.

[41] *Tr*, III, 1703–4.

[42] *Mythologicon*, p. 638, in A. van Staveren, ed., *Auctores Mythographi Latini.*

[43] In G. H. Bode, ed., *Scriptores Rerum Mythicarum*, pp. 36, 81, 202.

[44] *Confessio Amantis*, VII, 853–57, in G. C. Macaulay, ed., *Works of John Gower.* Cf. further J. P. Migne, ed., *Patrologia Latina*, XC, 1153.

the same time, the widespread dissemination of these two traditions, I have outlined them in the appendix.[45]

Both traditions are found together, however, with significant minor variations, in a popular work of the ninth century by Pseudo-Bede entitled *De Mundi Coelestis Terrestrisque Constitutione Liber:*

Sol secundum poetas dicitur in curru vehi quem trahunt equi, quorum haec sunt nomina, secundum Fulgentium. Primus, Erythros, id est, rubens, quia mane sol rubet. Secundus Acteon, id est, splendens, quia circa tertia clarius lucet. Tertius Lampon, id est, ardens; nam in meridie est fervidissimus. Quartus Philoges, id est, amans terram; nam nobis occidendo videtur appropriare.

Sed secundum Ovidium habet alia haec nomina: Eous, id est, oriens, vel surgens. Aethon, id est, elatus. Pyrois, id est, igneus: Phlegon, id est, acclivis, quia primum sol surgit, dehinc elevatur, postea fervet, in fine autem diei inclinatur ad occasum.[46]

It may be said at once that the evidence points to this passage as Henryson's exact source.

Only in the second paragraph of the quotation from Pseudo-Bede, referring to the Sun's horses *secundum Ovidium,* are the horses named in the exact order found in Henryson. Unique parallels occur in the individual characteristics of two of the horses: Henryson's first horse, "Callit Eoye, into the Orient," is similar to Pseudo-Bede's "Eous, id est, oriens"; and Henryson's third horse, "Peros, richt hait and richt fervent," copies Pseudo-Bede's "Pyrois . . . igneus . . . postea fervet." Further, Henryson's "sum deill ascendent" echoes the "elatus . . . dehinc elevatur" of Pseudo-Bede. These parallels to Henryson are found in no other version of the Sun's horses.

Turning to the name of the fourth horse, we see that the spelling "Philologie" or "Philologee" in Henryson's text derives from the

---

[45] See Appendix B.

[46] J. P. Migne, ed., *Patrologia Latina,* XC, 900. Concerning Pseudo-Bede, cf. J. L. E. Dreyer, "Mediaeval Astronomy," *Studies in the History and Method of Science,* ed. C. Singer, II, 106; P. Duhem, *Le Système du Monde,* III, 76 ff.; C. W. Jones, "Concepts of the Inferior Planets," *Isis,* XXIV (February, 1936), 397–99.

Fulgentian "Philoges" rather than the Ovidian "Phlegon." On this point the exigencies of riming may be invoked, for the form "Philoges" adapts itself, both in the number of syllables and potential end-rime, to Henryson's immediate purposes. It may be, therefore, that the poet, with Pseudo-Bede's *De Mundi* open before him, rejected the Ovidian spelling and went back a few lines to the Fulgentian form. This would explain the mixture of the two traditions in Henryson, establish the source of the passage, and solve the textual problem.

V

Henryson gives the following description of Venus (ll. 218–38):

Venus was thair present that goddes [gay],
Hir Sonnis querrell for to defend and mak
Hir awin complaint, cled in ane nyce array,
The ane half grene, the uther half Sabill black;
Quhyte hair as gold kemmit and sched abak;
Bot in hir face semit greit variance,
Quhyles perfyte treuth, and quhyles Inconstance

Under smyling scho was dissimulait,
Provocative, with blenkis Amorous,
And suddanely changit and alterait,
Angrie as ony Serpent vennemous
Richt pungitive, with wordis odious,
Thus variant scho was, quha list tak keip,
With ane Eye lauch, and with the uther weip.

In taikning that all fleschelie Paramour
Quhilk Venus hes in reull and governance,
Is sum tyme sweit, sum tyme bitter and sour
Richt unstabill, and full of variance,
Mingit with cairfull Joy and fals plesance,
Now hait, now cauld, now blyith, now full of wo,
Now grene as leif, now widderit and ago.

Unlike the preceding planet portraits, this portrait of Venus owes little to astrology. The mythological conception of Venus as the goddess of love is at the center of the characterization, but the emphasis has been thrown on her "greit variance," a quality which receives little or no stress in mythology or astrology. In his third stanza, the poet points out why his treatment is fitting, explaining that the inconstancy of Venus betokens the changing fortunes of love and lovers. Since the *Testament* is the story of the changing fortunes of two lovers, and since Venus is Cresseid's avowed goddess, Henryson's reason for varying the usual treatment may be easily understood.

In a passing allusion to the *Testament,* Professor Neilson remarks:

The description of Venus departs entirely from the tradition, all the stress being laid on her character: "Richt unstabill, and full of variance, Mingit with cairfull joy, and fals plesance." [47]

The poet, then, was striking out on a new path, but the direction of his efforts is incidentally revealed by the following observations of Professor Patch:

As early as the eleventh or twelfth century the similarity between Fortune and Love had been recognized . . . But some writers make a distinction between Love and Fortune, representing one as obstructing the work of the other, or making them at odds somehow, or at least not in complete union . . . Fortune and Love become associated in work, however. They are both accused of causing trouble for lovers, and their names are linked. In *Li Romanz de la Poire* . . . the Court of Love has become practically the Court of Fortune . . . In the *Panthère d'Amours,* and in the *Kingis Quair,* Fortune seems to be in complete control. Cases of love are finally referred to her decision, and the Court of Fortune appears to be an established fact . . . This identification of the two figures of Fortune and Love only means that they had much in common, and that in one aspect Fortune was certainly regarded as concerned with the affairs of love.[48]

Henryson's Venus is an example of the merging of the two personifications.

[47] W. A. Neilson, *The Origins and Sources of the Court of Love,* p. 160.

[48] H. R. Patch, *The Goddess Fortuna in Mediaeval Literature,* pp. 90–98. Cf. further, E. Sieper, ed., *Lydgate's Reson and Sensuallyte,* ll. 1547–54, 3363–92, a reference suggested by Parr.

The nature of Henryson's source, however, may be indicated with a little more precision. In the *Book of the Duchess,* Chaucer describes Fortune at some length (ll. 617–20, 626–49):

My boldnesse ys turned to shame,
For fals Fortune hath pleyd a game
Atte ches with me, allas! the while!
The trayteresse fals and ful of gyle

. . . . . .

An ydole of fals portrayture
Ys she, for she wol sone wrien;
She is the monstres hed ywrien,
As fylthe over-ystrawed with floures.
Hir moste worshippe and hir flour ys
To lyen, for that ys hyr nature;
Withoute feyth, lawe, or mesure
She ys fals; and ever laughynge
With oon eye, and that other wepynge.
That ys broght up, she set al doun.
I lykne hyr to the scorpioun,
That ys a fals, flaterynge beste;
For with his hed he maketh feste,
But al amydde hys flaterynge
With hys tayle he wol stynge
And envenyme; and so wol she.
She ys th'envyouse charite
That ys ay fals, and semeth wel,
So turneth she hyr false whel
Aboute, for hyt ys nothyng stable,
Now by the fire, now at table;
For many oon hath she thus yblent.
She ys pley of enchauntement,
That semth oon and ys not soo.

Henryson's Venus is essentially the same characterization: Chaucer says "for she wol sone wrien," and the Scot says "Thus variant scho was"; Chaucer likens Fortune to a scorpion who will "stynge and envenyme," while Henryson refers to a "Serpent vennemous Richt pungitive"; both poets assert that she laughs with one eye and weeps with the other; and while Chaucer calls Fortune's wheel "nothyng stable," Henryson speaks of Venus' rule as "Richt unstabill." In short, the Scot's portrait of Venus, like Chaucer's description of Fortune, consists of a series of variations upon the theme of inconstancy.[49] The appropriateness of this characterization needs little comment.[50]

VI

Henryson describes Mercury as follows (ll. 239–52, 264–70):

> With buik in hand than come Mercurius,
> Richt Eloquent, and full of Rethorie,
> With polite termis and delicious,
> With pen and Ink to report al reddie,
> Setting sangis and singand merilie:
> His Hude was reid, heklit atouir his Croun,
> Lyke to ane Poeit of the auld fassoun.
>
> Boxis he bair with fine Electuairis,
> And sugerit Syropis for digestioun,
> Spycis belangand to the Pothecairis,
> With mony hailsum sweit Confectioun,

[49] Other but less pertinent descriptions of Fortune occur in Boethius, *De Consolatione*, Bk. II, 1 ff., and Chaucer's *Romaunt*, ll. 5403 ff. The description of Venus in classical mythology bears little resemblance to Henryson's portrait. Cf. *Aeneid*, I, 402–5; *Fasti*, IV, 91 ff. Nor does the description found in the mythographers and encyclopedists. Cf. Albricus, *De Deorum Imaginibus*, in A. van Staveren, ed., *Auctores Mythographi Latini*, pp. 903–4, and Bartholomaeus Anglicus, *op. cit.*, Bk. VIII, chap. xxvi. Cf. further, E. Sieper, ed., Lydgate's *Reson and Sensuallyte*, ll. 1547–54, 3363–92. The astrologers place no emphasis upon the inconstancy of the planet, but rather describe Venus in terms of cold and moist qualities which exert a consistently similar influence. Cf. Albumasar, *op. cit.*, sig. h₅, and Lilly, *op. cit.*, pp. 72–76. Cf. further Panofsky, *op. cit.*, p. 26.

[50] It may be remembered that the plot of the *Testament* is more mythological than astrological in conception: deserted by Diomede, Cresseid blames Venus and Cupid, who, in return for her devotion, had promised her success in love; her criticism is called a blasphemy by Cupid, and she is judged, condemned, and punished on that ground. In the case of Venus, therefore, there is some reason to portray her in terms of the well-worn personification of mythology, since it would be more effective to have Cresseid blaspheme a goddess than a planet.

Doctour in Phisick cled in ane Skarlot goun,
And furrit weill, as sic ane aucht to be,
Honest and gude, and not ane word culd le.

. . . . .

Thus quhen thay gadderit war, thir Goddess sevin,
Mercurius thay cheisit with ane assent
To be foirspeikar in the Parliament.

Quha had bene thair, and liken for to heir
His facound toung, and termis exquisite,
Of Rethorick the prettick he micht leir,
In brief Sermone ane pregnant sentence wryte.

It is Mercury, too, who asks Cupid the cause of the convocation, and suggests that Saturn and Cynthia judge Cresseid (ll. 271–73, 295–300).

The astrological nature of the poet's description may be indicated by the following passage from Lilly:

Being well dignified, he represents a man of subtill and politick braine, intellect, and cogitation; an excellent disputant or Logician, arguing with learning and discretion, and using much eloquence in his speech, a searcher into all kinds of Mysteries and Learning, sharp and witty, learning almost any thing without a Teacher; ambitious of being exquisite in every Science . . . He generally signifies all literated men, Philosophers . . . Merchants, Secretaries, Scriveners . . . Poets, Orators, Advocates, Schoolmasters, Stationers, Printers . . . Atturneys . . . Clerks . . . Solicitors.[51]

The similarity of this passage to Henryson's portrait is evident: where Lilly calls Mercury "an excellent disputant," Henryson refers twice to Mercury's powers of "Rhetorick"; Lilly mentions Mercury's "eloquence in his speech," a characteristic which Henryson stresses, speaking of the planet as "Richt Eloquent . . . With polite termis and delicious"; Lilly says that Mercury is "sharp and witty," and the Scot expresses the same idea by his phrase "facound toung"; finally, Lilly likens Mercury to a scrivener and Henryson describes him as ready

[51] *Op. cit.*, pp. 77–78.

with pen and ink, while both associate the planet with poets.[52]

Although Mercury is seldom or never associated with medicine in the usual descriptions of that god or planet, Henryson portrays him as a doctor.[53] In so doing, the poet was apparently influenced by the *Canterbury Tales* (ll. 411, 422, 425–26):

> With us ther was a DOCTOUR OF PHISIK
>
> ·　·　·　·　·
>
> He was a verray, parfit praktisour
>
> ·　·　·　·　·
>
> Ful redy hadde he his apothecaries
> To sende hym drogges and his letuaries.

The parallel to Henryson is close, from the general attitude of approval to the phrase "Doctour in Phisick" and the specific words "Pothecairis" and "Electuairis" which appear in the *Testament*. Again, Chaucer's "Syngynge he was . . . He koude songes make and wel endite," referring to the Squire (*CT,* ll. 91, 95), may have suggested the Scot's "Setting sangis and singand merilie." [54] Of Mercury's apparel, the headpiece was a poetic convention and may be found in portraits of Chaucer,[55] while the well-furred scarlet gown betokened a person of great importance in the poet's day.[56] All in all, the portrait of Mercury is one of Henryson's happiest creations.

---

[52] For further astrological descriptions of Mercury similar to Lilly, cf. Pruckner, ed., *Ptolemaei . . . Quadripartitum,* pp. 6, 31, 50, 58; Firmicus, *Matheseos,* Pruckner's edition, p. 23; Albohazen, *op. cit.,* sig. a₅, *verso.* Cf. further Panofsky, *op. cit.,* p. 26.

[53] The connection between Mercury and medicine is tenuous, although it is possible to find some relationship: Mercury sometimes assumed the attributes of Hermes, and the latter is occasionally associated with medicine. Cf. *Dictionary of Greek and Roman Biography and Mythology,* ed. W. Smith (Boston, 1849), *s.v. Mercury* and *Hermes.* In classical mythology, Mercury is the god of cunning and theft, merchants and thieves, and he remains the same in the Middle Ages. Cf. Bartholomaeus Anglicus, *op. cit.,* Bk. VIII, chap. xxvii. In our day, the caduceus of Mercury (two snakes) has been mistakenly adopted by the Army Medical Corps instead of the rod of Aesculapius (one snake).

[54] The association of Mercury with music is traditional. Cf. Gower's *Confessio Amantis,* IV, 3332 ff.; Lydgate's *Troy Book, op. cit.,* II, 5604–8; and, of course, Ovid.

[55] Cf. G. G. Smith, *op. cit.,* I, 48.

[56] P. H. Brown, *Scotland before 1700* (Edinburgh, 1893), p. 27.

VII

Henryson's description of Cynthia is the shortest and the least original of the planet portraits (ll. 253–63):

> Nixt efter him come Lady Cynthia,
> The last of all, and swiftest in hir Spheir,
> Of colour blak, buskit with hornis twa,
> And in the nicht scho listis best appeir.
> Haw as the Leid, of colour nathing cleir;
> For all hir licht scho borrowis at hir brother
> Titan, for of hir self scho hes nane uther.
>
> Hir gyse was gray, and ful of spottis blak,
> And on hir breist ane Churle paintit full evin,
> Beirand ane bunche of Thornis on his bak,
> Quhilk for his thift micht clim na nar the hevin.

Having been appointed with Saturn to judge Cresseid, Cynthia descends from her seat and reads a "bill" stating that Cresseid is now deprived of her bodily heat and describing her leprous fate in detail (ll. 330–43).

The only astrological touch in the poet's treatment of Cynthia is his selection of this planet to assist in conferring the verdict of leprosy upon Cresseid. In general, the portrait is an amalgam of commonplaces. Many of the details which Henryson selects may be found in the following passage from Pliny:

But the wonder of everyone is vanquished by the last star, the one most familiar to the earth, and devised by nature to serve as a remedy for the shadows of darkness—the moon . . . always waxing and waning, and now curved into the horns of a sickle, now just halved in size, now rounding into a circle; spotted and then suddenly shining clear . . . The moon then is nearest to the pole, and therefore has the smallest orbit . . . she is governed by the sun's radiance as are the rest of the stars, as in fact she shines with a light entirely borrowed from him . . . She is sometimes seen spotted.[57]

[57] *Natural History,* tr. H. Rackham (London, 1938–40), I, 193–97.

Pliny's allusions to the moon's horns, her spots, and the statement that she receives her light from the sun, as well as the association with darkness and the implication that she is swift, have their counterpart in the *Testament* and elsewhere.[58] The reference in Henryson to the "Churle" on the moon's breast, or the man in the moon, is a commonplace.[59] In short, the poet gives a thoroughly conventional portrait of the moon.

Reviewing Henryson's treatment and description of the seven planets in the *Testament of Cresseid,* we may conclude that in general the Scot exercised considerable originality and perception by discarding for the most part the ancient mythological qualities of the gods and substituting the astrological qualities of the planets in which his age believed. In so doing, he was following Chaucer's example and conferring realism upon his narration. Specifically, Henryson appears to be indebted to astrological works such as Albohazen's *Liber de fatis astrorum,* although he added a variety of details from other sources with a total result that is well integrated and effective. Thus, five of the seven planets—Saturn, Jupiter, Mars, Phoebus, and Mercury—are fundamentally astrological in conception; Venus is portrayed with the emphasis upon her inconstancy, for poetic and dramatic reasons; and Cynthia, alone, is described in a rather conventional manner. The greatest single source of supplemental detail appears to be Chaucer, with lesser borrowings from Ovid, the *Romance of the Rose,* Lydgate, Pseudo-Bede, and others. None of these sources, however, is imitated slavishly, and Henryson deserves full credit for creating a series of powerful and compelling portraits.

[58] Typical allusions to the moon's horns occur in Boethius, *De Consolatione,* III, *m.* 6, and the *Kingis Quair,* ed. A. Lawson, p. 3. Allusions to the fact that the moon's light is borrowed from the sun occur in *Le Roman de la Rose,* ed. E. Langlois, IV, 16843 ff., and Gower, *Confessio Amantis,* in Macaulay, ed., *Complete Works,* III, 253. The moon's swiftness is emphasized in astrology. Cf. Lilly, *op. cit.,* pp. 81 ff.

[59] The man in the moon is said to be first mentioned by Neckham: T. Wright, ed., *De Natura Rerum,* p. xviii. A passage which resembles Henryson occurs in Pecock: C. Babington, ed., *Repressor,* I, 155. Cf. further Langlois, ed., *Le Roman de la Rose,* IV, 16881 ff., and *Troilus and Criseyde,* I, 1023–24.

Chapter VI

THE MEETING OF THE LOVERS

ONE PASSAGE in the *Testament of Cresseid* has been singled out consistently for high praise: the meeting of the lovers. William Godwin was perhaps the first to comment on it:

In the single instance of the state of mind, the half-recognition, half-ignorance, attributed to Troilus in his last encounter with Creseide, there is a felicity of conception impossible to be surpassed.[1]

Nearly a century later, George Saintsbury remarked that "the stanzas describing this situation are nearly perfect." [2] In 1926, Professor Manley praised the passage highly if obliquely by referring to a few lines in the *Pardoner's Tale* which, he wrote, achieved "an intensity and impressiveness attained again only once in the next two-hundred years—and then not in English but in the lowland Scotch of Robert Henryson's amazing picture of the meeting of Troilus and the abject figure of her who once was Cressida." [3] More recently, Professor G. P. Krapp wrote:

There is one fine moment in the poem, when Troilus riding by with a company of his knights returning to Troy after a successful raid, sees Cressida standing by the roadside among other lepers, with her begging bowl in her hand. A flash of memory but not of recognition, brightens in him for a moment, he throws a gift of money to her, and rides on his way without a word.[4]

Such comments could be multiplied.[5]

[1] W. Godwin, *Life of Geoffrey Chaucer* (London, 1803), I, 313.
[2] Saintsbury, *A Short History of English Literature,* p. 184.
[3] J. M. Manley, *Some New Light on Chaucer* (New York, 1926), pp. 289–90.
[4] G. P. Krapp, *Troilus and Cressida* (New York, 1932), p. xiv.
[5] Cf. G. Bullett, "The Fortunes of Cressida," *New Statesman,* XXI (1923), 362–63;

The stanzas which induced these remarks are as follows (ll. 498–511):

> Than upon him scho kest up baith hir Ene,
> And with ane blenk it come into his thocht,
> That he sumtime hir face befoir had sene,
> Bot scho was in sic plye he knew hir nocht,
> Yit than hir luik into his mynd it brocht
> The sweit visage and amorous blenking
> Of fair Cresseid sumtyme his awin darling.
>
> Na wonder was, suppois in mynd that he
> Tuik hir figure sa sone, and lo now quhy?
> The Idole of ane thing, in cace may be
> Sa deip Imprentit in the fantasy
> That it deludis the wittis outwardly,
> And sa appeiris in forme and lyke estait,
> Within the mynd as it was figurait.[6]

The first of these two stanzas describes the situation when the lovers meet; the second furnishes an explanation of it. The key to the situation that the poet is describing occurs in the last five lines, which give a compact summary of a specific psychological process.[7]

The process which Henryson summarizes may be traced back at least as far as Aristotle. Aristotle's psychology is set forth in his *De anima* and his *Parva naturalia,* where he outlines his theory of cognition.[8] The pertinent elements of this theory may be summarized

---

W. J. Courthope, *A History of English Poetry* (New York, 1895–1910), I, 369; W. P. Ker, *Form and Style in Poetry,* pp. 85–87; H. M. R. Murray, ed., *Selected Fables, The Testament of Cresseid and Robene and Makyne,* p. 10; R. K. Gordon, *The Story of Troilus,* p. xvii.

[6] H. H. Wood, ed., *The Poems and Fables of Robert Henryson,* p. 122.

[7] The word *psychology* is used here in its primary sense of a science which treats of the mind in any of its aspects.

[8] Cf. W. A. Hammond, ed., *Aristotle's Psychology,* pp. xv–lxxxvi; W. D. Ross, *Aristotle,* pp. 129–53; and G. S. Brett, *A History of Psychology,* I, 100 ff. Incidental mention of Aristotle's psychology and its influence in the Middle Ages occurs in L. Ambrosi, *La Psicologia della Immaginazione nella Storia Filosofia,* pp. 6–60; B. Schweitzer, "Der bildende Künstler und der Begriff des Künstlerischen," *Neue Heidelberger Jahrbücher,* 1925, pp. 28–132; and M. W. Bundy, *The Theory of Imagina-*

as follows: the process of knowing is accomplished in three steps— sensation, imagination, and rational thought.[9] The first step, sensation, is the stimulation of the sense organs by objects external to the body.[10] The second step, imagination, has the function of storing copies of these sense-impressions in the mind after the external object has been removed.[11] Thus, the imagination is a storehouse of images.[12] These images may be recalled deliberately or spontaneously through the process of recollection, which operates according to the laws of association.[13] Aristotle terms this process the function of the reproductive imagination.[14] The third step, rational thought, includes the power of discriminating between the true and the false.[15] When this power is disturbed by passion, illusions may result.[16]

Discussing illusions in connection with this theory of imagination, Aristotle says:

After the removal of the external sensible object, the experienced sensations persist. To this we must add that when under the influence of strong feeling we are easily deceived regarding our sensations, different persons in different ways, as e.g. the coward under the influence of fear and the lover under that of love have such illusions that the former owing to a trifling

---

tion in Classical and Mediaeval Thought, pp. 60 ff., 146 ff. These scholars are concerned primarily with tracing the origins of modern definitions of imagination, a problem which does not concern us here.

[9] De anima, 428a 8 ff. and De memoria, 449b 5 ff. Cf. further Hammond, op. cit., pp. lvi ff.

[10] De anima, 424a ff.

[11] De anima, 429a 21 ff. Cf. further Hammond, ed., Aristotle's Psychology, pp. lvi ff.

[12] Cf. ibid., pp. lvi–lvii.

[13] For an exposition of the process of recollection, operating according to the laws of association, cf. De memoria, 451b 6 ff. For the distinction between deliberate and spontaneous recollection, cf. De memoria, 453a 26 ff.

[14] According to Aristotle, the imagination functions in a double capacity; in addition to the reproductive or retentive function mentioned above, it also has a productive or creative function. The productive function creates new images which have only a subjective existence and thus accounts for artistic creation as well as delirium. Cf. Hammond, ed., Aristotle's Psychology, pp. lix ff. We are concerned only with the retentive function.

[15] Cf. ibid., p. lxiv.

[16] Cf. De anima, 424a ff.; De memoria, 449b 5 ff.; De somno, 460b 15 ff.

resemblance thinks he sees an enemy and the latter his beloved. And the more impressionable the person is, the less is the resemblance required. Similarly everybody is easily deceived when in anger or influenced by any strong desire, and the more subject one is to these feelings the more one is deceived.[17]

This example of the lover under the influence of love, who thinks he sees his beloved because of a trifling resemblance, is strikingly similar to Henryson's Troilus, who is reminded of the fair Cresseid by the leper, with the exception that in the *Testament* the leper happens to be Cresseid.

Turning back to the last five lines of the poet's second stanza, we may observe that Henryson's "Idole" is the equivalent of Aristotle's copy of a sense-impression which persists in the mind after the external object has been removed.[18] "Idole" refers to the image of the fair Cresseid in the mind of Troilus. Since the poet's "fantasy" is the same faculty as Aristotle's imagination,[19] when Henryson states that the "Idole" may be "deip Imprentit in the fantasy," he is emphasizing the image-storing function of the imagination. Thus the resulting delusion of the "wittis" or rational thought is caused by Troilus' passion for his beloved, and in his mind he sees the "Idole" or image of fair Cresseid in the "forme" or bodily likeness that it was "figurait" or imagined.[20]

Applying the Aristotelian theory of cognition to Henryson's first

[17] *De somno*, 460*b* 15 ff.

[18] The *NED* gives *image* as one of the meanings of *idol*, adding, "a mental fiction; a phantasy or fancy." No examples are given until well after Henryson's time. Aristotle rarely uses the word "idol" in the sense that Henryson does, and it seems probable that the poet was translating LL. *idolum*.

[19] The terms *fantasy* and *imagination* were used interchangeably in the Middle Ages. See Bundy, *op. cit.*, p. 266. The *NED* definies *fantasy* as "Imagination; the process or the faculty of forming mental representations of things not actually present." Aristotle uses the word *phantasia* to refer to the faculty of imagination. Cf. Hammond, ed., *Aristotle's Psychology*, p. lvii. He also uses it to refer to the product of the imagination, although his usual term is *phantasm*.

[20] See G. G. Smith, ed., *Poems of . . . Robert Henryson*, I, 113. Cf. further *NED*, *s.v. Figure*.

stanza, in which he describes what takes place when the lovers meet, we see that the "luik" or expression of the leper-woman, as she casts up "baith hir Ene," constitutes the trifling resemblance mentioned by Aristotle. This trifling resemblance (which the poet is careful to say did not lead to recognition, although it is sufficient to make Troilus think he has seen the leper before) initiates a spontaneous process of recollection whereby the leper recalls to Troilus the "sweit visage and amorous blenking of fair Cresseid." It is this image which Troilus' reason, disturbed by passion, cannot distinguish from the leper-woman before him.[21] In brief, the actual object of his sight is blotted out by the image of his beloved, and Troilus thinks for a moment that he actually sees his fair Cresseid. A moment later he comes to his senses and rides on.

It is perhaps unnecessary at this point to remark that the modern reader's usual interpretation of Henryson's stanzas, namely, that Troilus is reminded of his beloved by someone who is to all intents and purposes unknown to him, falls short of the poet's intended meaning. Henryson is describing a far more subtle and complex situation in which something much nearer to actual recognition takes place.[22]

[21] A word may be added concerning ll. 505-6. A minor problem of interpretation hinges upon the meaning of the word *figure,* which may be glossed as "bodily appearance" or "mental image." See G. G. Smith, ed., *Poems of . . . Henryson,* I, 113. In either case, the poet's emphasis is upon the fact that Troilus took her *figure* in mind *sa sone,* i.e., quickly or hastily (*ibid.,* I, 158), and Henryson's intention is to lend credibility to his explanation by stressing the precipitance either of the meeting itself or of the psychological processes involved. Thus, the lines might mean: (1) that Troilus looked at the leper-woman hastily, or (2) that the mental image of the fair Cresseid was recalled to the mind of Troilus quickly. In the light of the poet's careful use of Aristotelian psychology, the latter interpretation seems preferable. Chaucer, for example, uses the word to signify a mental image. See *Tr,* I, 366.

There is the additional but less important problem of whether the word *suppois* is used as a verb or conjunction. If a verb, no change in the punctuation is necessary, and a needless duplication of conjunctions is avoided. It would then be possible to paraphrase *suppois in mynd* as "bear in mind," i.e., as words addressed to the reader.

[22] John Buchan, for example, is understandably mistaken when he says that Troilus actually recognized Cresseid. Cf. *A History of English Literature,* p. 36.

Although it is possible that Henryson is directly indebted to Aristotle, whose works were available in Latin translation long before the poet's time,[23] Henryson's statement of theory (ll. 507–11) emphasizes a factor which is not emphasized by Aristotle.[24] Aristotle says that an impression takes place, while Henryson amplifies this statement by stressing the depth of the impression. Thus, in the *Testament,* the verb "Imprentit" is modified by the phrase "sa deip" (l. 508). That some such extension of Aristotle's theories was current long before Henryson is evident from the following passage in Plutarch:

Neither, as one was pleased to say, are poetical fancies, by reason of their lively expressions, rightly called waking dreams; but the dialogues of persons enamored, discoursing with their absent loves, and dallying, embracing, and expostulating with them as if they were present, much rather deserve this name. For the sight seems to delineate other fancies in the water, that quickly glide away and slip out of the mind; whereas the imaginations of lovers, being as it were enamelled by fire, leave the images of things imprinted in the memory, moving, living, speaking, and remaining for a long time.[25]

Here the typical thoughts and actions of lovers are ascribed to the intensity with which the image of the beloved is imprinted in the

---

[23] Cf. A. Jourdain, *Recherches critiques sur l'age et l'origine des traductions latines d'Aristote,* pp. 21 ff.; and L. J. Paetow, *A Guide to the Study of Medieval History* (New York, 1931), pp. 425–26. Aristotle is mentioned twice by Henryson. Cf. H. H. Wood, ed., *Poems and Fables of . . . Henryson,* pp. 58 (l. 1636), 189 (l. 17).

[24] In general, the Aristotelian tradition of the psychology of the imagination, with its incidental mention of illusions, forms a dominant trend in the Middle Ages, and various authors emphasized various elements in the tradition. Thus the Stoics in general, and Epictetus in particular, aided by the ethical bent of Platonism, stressed the connection between imagination and illusion; Plutarch brought out the relationship of imagination with the theory of humors; Macrobius stressed the connection with dreams. The same psychology is found with minor variations in a succession of influential authors, among them Boethius, Augustine, Avicenna, John of Salisbury, Averroes, Albertus Magnus, Roger Bacon, Bonaventura, and Thomas Aquinas. Cf. Bundy, *op. cit.,* pp. 172 ff. It should be remembered that these statements of Aristotelian psychology are metaphysical, not literary.

[25] W. W. Godwin, tr., *Plutarch's Morals,* IV, 280.

memory by the imagination. This particular process became the most widely adopted device of the Aristotelian tradition in the literature of the Middle Ages. It may be found, applied in various ways to varying situations, in the *Roman de Troie*,[26] *Le Roman de la Rose*,[27] Boccaccio's *Fiametta*,[28] Dante's *Vita Nuova*,[29] Chaucer's works,[30] and elsewhere.[31]

Henryson employs other terms which embody further distinctions which Aristotle does not stress. Thus the poet refers to what takes place outwardly in contrast to what takes place inwardly, saying that the wits are deluded outwardly by the "Idole," which appears "in forme and lyke estait" as imagined inwardly (ll. 507–10). This distinction appears in Augustine, who made the first great Christian synthesis of Aristotelian psychology.[32] Augustine writes, in his *De Trinitate*:

Voluntas vero illa quae hac atque illac fert et refert aciem formandam, conjungitque formatam, si ad interiorem phantasiam tota confluxerit, atque a praesentia corporum quae circumjacent sensibus, atque ab ipsis sensibus corporis, animi aciem omnino averterit, atque ad eam quae intus cernitur imaginem penitus converterit; tanta offenditur similitudo speciei corporalis expressa ex memoria, ut nec ipsa ratio discernere sinatur, utrum foris corpus ipsum videatur, an intus tale aliquid cogitetur . . . Et memini me audisse a quodam, quod tam expressam et quasi solidam speciem feminei corporis in cogitando cernere soleret, ut ei se quasi misceri sentiens, etiam genitalibus flueret.[33]

[26] L. Constans, ed., *Le Roman de Troie par Benoît de Sainte-Maure*, III, 146–47.

[27] E. Langlois, ed., *Le Roman de la Rose*, IV, 226 (ll. 18357–63).

[28] I. Moutier, ed., *Opere Volgari*, VI, 9.

[29] *Opere di Dante Alighieri*, ed. E. Moore, p. 205.

[30] Cf. *Tr*, I, 295–98, 365–66; III, 1541–44, 1499–1502. Cf. further *MerchT*, ll. 1577–79, 1977–81; *MillT*, ll. 3611–13; *CYT*, ll. 1071–73; *SqT*, ll. 371–72; and *HF*, ll. 36–40. Cf. my article, "A Note on Chaucer and Aristotelian Psychology," *Studies in Philology*, XLIII (January, 1946), 15–21.

[31] Cf. A. Lawson, ed., *The Kingis Quair*, p. 8; *Confessio Amantis*, in G. C. Macaulay, ed., *Works of John Gower*, II, 311–12; *Fabula Duorum Mercatorum*, ed. H. N. MacCracken, *op. cit.*, II, 497–98.

[32] Cf. M. W. Bundy, *op. cit.*, pp. 264–65; M. Ferraz, *De la Psychologie de Saint Augustin* (Paris, 1862), *passim*.

[33] J. P. Migne, ed., *Patrologia Latina* (Paris, 1844–64), XLII, 989 (Bk. XI, cap. iv).

Henryson may be making use of the Augustinian version of this particular concept since, in addition to the similar distinction between the body seen outside and something of the kind thought of within,[34] Augustine's phrase "tanta offenditur similitudo speciei corporalis" stresses the same detail as Henryson's statement that the "Idole . . . sa appeiris in Forme and lyke estait." Further, it is interesting that Augustine gives an example of someone who thought he saw a female body and was moved as if it were reality: the experience of Troilus in the *Testament* (ll. 512–18) is similar.

Some light may be thrown upon the tradition in which Henryson was writing by distinguishing it from other traditions. There seems to be little or no connection, for example, between this Aristotelian process and the even more conventional device whereby "an affluence, sometimes figured as a spear or arrow, passed from the lady's eyes through those of the lover into his heart."[35] Chaucer employs both devices on different occasions, but the Aristotelian device is psychological, concerning itself with the working of the imagination, in technical terms, and resulting in a variety of effects; the other device is physiological, concerning itself with the working of the heart, in popular terms, and resulting solely in love. The similarity of the two devices lies chiefly in the fact that both are used to explain the manner of falling in love.

Again, the process with which we are concerned appears to be independent of the courtly love tradition. No trace of it has been found in Ovid. In the *De Arte Honeste Amandi* of Andreas Capellanus, the only reference that even suggests Aristotle is the mention,

---

[34] Henryson's emphasis on what takes place outwardly and inwardly is more reminiscent of Augustine than may at first appear, for the latter's theory of cognition consists of successive groups of three factors, or trinities: the first is the trinity of the outward man, the second of the inward man. Cf. *De Trinitate,* Lib. XI, cap. 1 ff. No hint of the ethical factor of the will, upon which Augustine places so much emphasis, is found in the *Testament.* Cf. further Bundy, *op. cit.,* pp. 157 ff.

[35] Cf. F. N. Robinson, ed., *The Complete Works of Geoffrey Chaucer,* p. 773, note to l. 1096.

in the opening pages, of "excessive meditation" as one of the various causes of love.[36] An examination of *The Dove's Neck-Ring,* which expounds the Moorish conception of love and which probably influenced the troubadours, reveals nothing pertinent.[37] Nor has the device been found in the poetry of the troubadours. The Aristotelian tradition appears to have coexisted with other traditions without losing its identity and with sufficient vitality to be employed with great accuracy by Henryson.

Henryson's use of Aristotelian psychology is the most sophisticated that I have discovered. His exact source for the stanzas describing the meeting of the lovers probably cannot be identified, but it seems clear that he went to some precise statement of the process as it is found in Aristotle, Plutarch, or Augustine, or more likely, a later author who combined all three. Since this material was one of the divisions of the Three Philosophies in the university curriculum, we are justified in concluding that here is further evidence that the poet may have been a teacher.

The poet's accomplishment may be more precisely estimated. The chance meeting of the lovers offers a situation crowded with dramatic potentialities, and a lesser poet might have been unable to resist the temptation to have recognition take place with a great amount of moral *sentence* delivered by the principal characters. On the contrary, the poet's treatment is remarkably restrained and effective, and the fact that Troilus' experience is caused by the sight of Cresseid herself, although she is unrecognizable, is a brilliant touch. The irony of the situation depends on the fact that recognition does not take place, but the suspense of the situation is increased by the fact that recognition very nearly occurs. To achieve this poignant climax, Henryson made an original and strikingly successful use of Aristotelian psychology.

[36] Cf. J. J. Parry, ed., *The Art of Courtly Love by Andreas Capellanus,* p. 28.

[37] Cf. A. R. Nykl, ed., *A Book containing the Risāla known as* The Dove's Neck-Ring *about Love and Lovers, passim.*

Chapter VII

THE POET AS HUMANITARIAN

*I*N THE PRECEDING CHAPTERS I have been chiefly concerned with Henryson's times, the origins of his poetry, and the manner in which he made use of his sources. By way of applying some part of this material, I should like to offer a few conjectures on the poet as an individual. It may be that Kinaston's doubtful anecdote about the dying Henryson, rejecting with amused skepticism the suggestion that he employ an incantation to cure his "fluxe," epitomizes the poet. For with fifteenth-century Scotland as a frame of reference, Henryson may be characterized as a realist of considerable insight and integrity, employing a salty wit to expose the shams of his day. His compassion for the downtrodden, however, makes him more than simply an amused skeptic, for essentially he is a humanitarian in the best sense of the word, reserving his satire for minor abuses while thundering with electric wrath at "wrangous" injustice.

The poet's outstanding technique and craftsmanship—the easy flow of his narrative, his metrical fluency and variety, and his skillful creation of tone and atmosphere—have been ably discussed elsewhere.[1] Accordingly, I should like to limit the present chapter to a short exposition of internal evidence in Henryson's poetry which points to a constant factor in the poet's general attitude, namely, his championship of the peasantry.

Fifteenth-century Scotland was an age of transition from a feudal to a mercantile or money economy. Violence was the rule, aided by devastating plagues, an erratic central authority, and the continual

---

[1] Cf. G. G. Smith, *The Poems of Robert Henryson*, I, xiv ff.

changing of land from hand to hand as a result of ceaseless feuds. In this way, many of the less powerful landed gentry were dispossessed upon the reversion of their land to a new overlord. Feudal services were being commuted into money payments, and arable land was being forcibly converted into more profitable sheep pasturage by the feudal lords. To this increasing pool of dispossessed peasants and gentry, the slogan of loyalty, whether feudal or tribal, was beginning to have a hollow ring since it symbolized an arrangement which no longer protected them. Meanwhile, the towns were prospering if the countryside was not, and the merchants and craftsmen, aided by their guilds, were obtaining hitherto unknown economic advantages. On all these facets of the times, Henryson has something to say, and his attitude is both discernible and revealing.

Henryson observed the life around him with a keen, kindly, and sometimes indignant eye. The chief fruits of his observation may be found in his version of Aesop's *Fables*. At the outset, the poet suggests that it is profitable to mingle "merie sport" among earnest subjects, "to light the spreit, and gar the tyme be schort." Not that Henryson cannot moralize with high seriousness and fire when he so desires. But in his *Fables* he relegates most of his moral *sentence* to the end of each story, and it is difficult to escape the impression that he intends his fables to be at least as entertaining as they are instructive.

The poet's treatment of character in the *Fables* sheds light on his general attitude.[2] While he denounces the grasping nobility and the corrupt clergy who prey upon the peasant, the poet's attitude toward the rising townspeople, who were not yet in a position to take advantage of the peasantry, varies from one of chilliness to one of gleeful derision. Henryson's warmth, tenderness, and compassion are reserved for the peasants; nor does his sympathy deteriorate to a mawkish sentimentality, for his "sempill folk" are a sturdily inde-

---

[2] In the following discussion of the *Fables*, I have omitted all mention of Henryson's sources, a subject competently treated by G. G. Smith, in *Poems of . . . Henryson*, I, xxix–xlv.

pendent lot. When wronged or even patronized, they are most vocal
and quick to expose the foul play or affectations of their opponents.

A hint of this prototype may be found in the fable of the *Cock and
the Jewel,* which tells of a poor Cock who finds a jewel in an ash
heap. The Cock is no aristocrat; he realizes at once that the jewel is
not for him. He addresses it, however, with the courtesy reserved for
his superiors, employing a variation of the time-honored *ubi-sunt*
device (ll. 79, 106–10):

> "O gentill Jasp! O riche and Nobill thing!
>
> . . . . .
>
> "Quhar suld thow mak thy habitatioun?
> Quhar suld thou dwell, bot in ane Royall Tour?
> Quhar suld thow sit, bot on ane Kingis Croun,
> Exaltit in worschip and in grit honour?
> Rise, gentill Jasp, of all stanis the flour . . ."

Although he frankly prefers corn to jewels, the Cock's courtesy is so
great that he suggests that the jewel has reason to despise him for
his plebeian tastes (ll. 90–91, 97–98):

> I lufe fer better thing of les availl,
> As draf, or corne, to fill my tume Intraill
>
> . . . . .
>
> And thow agane, Upon the samin wyis,
> For les availl may me as now dispyis.

The Cock thereupon deserts the jewel, remaining true to the logic
of his station in life, which the poet probably considered fitting and
proper.

The humor of the fable is one of situation—a sort of *noblesse oblige*
in reverse—but it is impossible not to sense the poet's amused sympathy with the poverty-stricken Cock's airy dismissal of the jewel
and his sturdily independent advocacy of the simple way of life. The
Cock also makes a very practical point (ll. 104–5):

> For houngrie men may not leve on lukis:
> Had I dry breid, I compt not for na cukis.

By this comment, which breaks right out of the Aesopic context, the poet makes it clear that beneath the surface of the Cock's amusing monologue lies a realistic attitude toward everyday life. The Cock is a poor person of character and integrity.

In the tale of the "Twa Myis," Henryson's sympathetic attitude toward the impoverished peasant becomes more evident in his characterization of the "rurall mous." At the same time, his coolness toward townspeople may be felt in his portrayal of the "burges mous." The very first words that the town Mouse utters can scarcely prejudice the reader in her favor: in a delighted flurry of hospitality at her older sister's visit, the country Mouse has just finished ransacking her cupboard to put together the best meal she can offer; the town Mouse, however, sniffing at her younger sister's rustic banquet of withered peas and nuts, disdainfully inquires, "Sister, is this your dayly fude?" and adds that it is "bot a scorne."

The country Mouse immediately bristles at her older sister's attempt to patronize her. Madame, she says, you are the more to blame; my mother said, Sister, when we were born, that you and I both lay within one womb; I keep the style and custom of my mother by living in poverty, for we have no lands. The town Mouse is unmoved: "My fair sister," she says, "have me excusit."

So the country Mouse switches resourcefully to higher moral grounds (ll. 232–38):

> "Quhat plesure is in the ffeistis delicate,
> The quhilkis ar gevin with ane glowmand brow?
> Ane gentill hart is better recreate
> With blyith curage, than seith to him ane Kow.
> Ane modicum is mair ffor till allow,
> Swa that gude will be kerver at the dais,
> Than thrawin vult and mony spycit mais."

For the first time, the town Mouse is a bit shaken by the moral conviction of her younger sister and sits sadly but quietly at the table, with "littill will to sing." After a short while, however, she can contain herself no longer (ll. 246–49):

> "Lat be this hole and cum into my place;
> I sall to you schaw be experience
> My gude friday is better nor your pace;
> My dische likingis is worth your haill expence."

As an added inducement, the city Mouse announces: "Off cat, nor fall trap, I have na dreid"—an ironic bit of foreshadowing.

The country Mouse is finally persuaded to leave her hovel, but the manner of her assent indicates a characteristic change in her attitude: "I grant," she says laconically; from this point on, she is no longer the gracious hostess but rather the grudging guest. The poet devotes two stanzas to a description of the fine food provided by the town Mouse, who asks her country sister if she notices the difference between this "chalmer and hir sarie nest." The reply of the country Mouse is a strong mixture of dourness and doom: "Ye dame . . . how lang will this lest?"

In spite of her reservations, the country Mouse rapidly learns to enjoy the pleasures of the town. In fact, she is singing "Haill Yule, Haill," when the steward opens the door. The mice flee, as the poet says, without tarrying to wash, but the steward does not notice them. The country Mouse, however, is very much upset, and only the "wordis hunny sweit" of her older sister can persuade her to get up from where she lies "flatling on the ground." At this juncture, the country Mouse is scarcely able to announce that starving in peace is better than a "feist in this dreid and diseis," but her opinions remain unshaken.

Just as the country Mouse has been persuaded to return to the table and drink "anis or twyse," the cat appears. The town Mouse darts to her hole, "as fyre on flint," but her younger sister is caught by "Gib hunter, our Jolie Cat, and her worst fears are realized (ll. 330–33):

> Fra fute to fute he kest hir to and ffra,
> Quhylis up, quhylis doun, als cant as ony kid;
> Quhylis wald he lat hir rin under the stra,
> Quhylis wald he wink, and play with hir buk heid.

(The poet, it may be noted, is writing with his eye on the object.) The country Mouse finally escapes and, pausing only to castigate town life, flees to her rural hovel.

The country Mouse is a real individual with characteristics that are both Scottish and universal. She is poor but proud in the functional sense that she is clever enough to convert her poverty into a source of pride. Her personality is precisely that which would appear in an intelligent person surrounded by the disadvantages of the country. Recognizing her position, she tends to overcompensate in minor ways. Thus, she adopts a few simple and safe convictions about which she is irrepressibly articulate and almost shrill. Hence the reiterated moralizing, the gruff reservations, and the touch of assertiveness. Nor is she above simply making points in an argument. Yet her rural skepticism is capable of rapid readjustment when the advantages are visible and immediate. And through it all glows a canny Scots dourness.

Henryson's keen insight into the character of the country Mouse is exceeded only by his evident affection for her, while his portrayal of the town Mouse, who is not only proud and overbearing but also contemptuous of her younger sister, suggests a mild dislike of the burgesses. As we have seen, the growing prosperity of the towns, with the various privileges available to the townsmen, offered a strong contrast to the poverty of the countryside, and the poet's attitude toward the town is in keeping with his identification of himself with the peasantry, a subject more fully discussed later.

In the fable of *The Fox, the Wolf, and the Cadger,* Henryson describes another member of the merchant group, the Cadger, showing less sympathy for him than for the town Mouse. The Fox and the Wolf, it appears, have no doubts about the stinginess of the Cadger as he comes along the road singing, his horse carrying fish-baskets full of herring to market (ll. 2037–39):

> Thocht we wald thig, yone verray Churlische chuff,
> He will not giff us ane hering off his Creill,
> Befoir yone Churle on kneis thocht we wald kneill.

So the Fox resorts to a trick: he plays dead in the middle of the road and waits for the Cadger to discover him.

Coming upon the Fox, the Cadger is highly pleased and very sensibly decides to make "mittennis tway" of the Fox's skin. Henryson describes the ecstatic delight of the Cadger with infectious gaiety (ll. 2060–62):

> He lap full lichtlie about him quhair he lay,
> And all the trace he trippit on his tais;
> As he had hard ane pyper play, he gais.

Further, the Cadger's monologue upon his own good luck is a nice bit of self-characterization (ll. 2063–69):

> "Heir lyis the Devyll" (quod he), "deid in ane dyke.
> Sic ane selcouth saw I not this sevin yeir;
> I trow ye have bene tussillit with sum tyke,
> That garris you ly sa still withouttin steir:
> Schir Foxe, in Faith, ye ar deir welcum heir;
> It is sum wyfis malisone, I trow,
> For pultrie pyking, that lychtit hes on yow."

Again, the Cadger's well-developed sense of property is suggested by his twice-repeated announcement that no peddler is going to steal this skin and ship it to Flanders—the customary port to which furs were exported. He takes the Fox by the heels and "with ane swak he swang him on the creillis," a line which suggests his businesslike zeal.

While the Fox is emptying the creel and the Wolf is collecting the herring, the Cadger walks happily along leading his horse and singing "Huntis up, up, upon hie." He discovers the trick a moment later. At this point in the fable, the reader is presented with a contrasting side of the Cadger's personality, the side that is uppermost when business is bad. The escaped Fox rubs salt into the wound (ll. 2096–97):

> "And sell thy hering thow hes thair till hie price,
> Ellis thow sall wyn nocht on thy merchandice."

The Cadger "trimillit for teyne," and he swears revenge. Nevertheless, with the objectivity of a man who has known responsibility and profited by it, he blames himself for not having a stick in hand to beat such rogues. With characteristic energy, he "lap out over ane dyke, And hakkit doun ane staff . . . That hevie wes and off the Holyne grene."

The Fox now returns to the Wolf and persuades him to try the same trick with tales of a "Nekhering" (the pun is intentional) in the Cadger's creel, too large for the Fox to lift and "callour, pypand lyke ane Petrik Ee." So the Wolf plays dead in the middle of the road and waits for the Cadger. Riding because the load is so light, the Cadger is nursing his wrath. When he spies the Wolf, however, his mercantile caution asserts itself (ll. 2175–76):

> "Softlie," he said, "I wes begylit anis;
> Be I begylit twyis, I schrew us baith . . ."

And the Cadger decides to beat the Wolf without any further investigation.

Henryson's characterization of the Cadger seems to be reasonably fair and true to life. In fact, this Cadger's alternating moods of joy and anger are motivated by sound business reasons. The poet implies that members of the merchant group are proverbially stingy, but he adds other details which are more revealing, such as the practical energy, the responsible self-criticism, and the instinctive caution even in anger. Add to this the flavor and bounce of the verse itself, and the result is a lively characterization tinged with keen satire. Henryson seems to have enjoyed making a cadger the butt of a part of his fable.

Of the few sympathetically described protagonists of the *Fables* who are not peasants, the character of the Fox, in the tale of *The Fox and the Wolf,* is of particular interest. In a sense, the "wylie tratour Tod" is out of character as, for the space of one fable, he appears to be simply an imaginative but confused person with an honest impulse to do the right thing. The poet, of course, is occupied with his trenchant criticism of the church, and the fable is Reynardian rather than Aesopic. Nevertheless, the characterization of the Fox has a logic of its own.

At the outset, the Fox studies the planets and is suddenly convinced that he is about to die. Remarking that the lot of "we thevis" is no better than that of the poor, the Fox goes in search of a confessor. He soon encounters "Freir Wolff Waitskaith" (one-who-waits-to-do-injury), and the Fox's complete, immediate faith in the Wolf, whom he traditionally is supposed to outwit, is almost touching (ll. 670–85):

> Seand this Wolff, this wylie tratour Tod
> On kneis fell, with hude in to his nek;
> "Welcome, my Gostlie ffather under God"
> (Quod he), with mony binge and mony bek.
> "Ha" (quod the Wolff), "Schir Tod, for quhat effek
> Mak ye sic feir? Ryse up, put on your hude."
> "Father" (quod he), "I haif grit cause to dude.
>
> "Ye ar Mirrour, Lanterne, and sicker way,
> Suld gyde sic sempill folk as me to grace.
> Your bair feit, and your Russet Coull off gray,
> Your lene cheik, your paill pietious face,
> Schawis to me your perfite halines.
> For weill wer him, that anis in his lyve
> Had hap to yow his sinnis ffor to schryve."
>
> "Na, selie Lowrence" (quod the Wolf), and leuch:
> "It plesis me that ye ar penitent."

Above and beyond the amusing description of the Wolf as a pious priest, the novelty of a Fox who not only cannot see through the Wolf's disguise but who also has convinced himself that he is one of the "sempill folk," suggests that Henryson may be diverging again from the beaten path of the Aesopic fabulist.

The conscientious integrity of the Fox during confession is remarkable. When asked by the Wolf if he is sorry for his trespasses, the Fox cannot honestly say that he is. The Wolf seems a little surprised but continues nevertheless, asking if the Fox will "forbeir in tyme to cum and mend." The Fox cannot agree to this, either, pointing out quite seriously that stealing is his means of livelihood, and adding that his social pretensions make it impossible to work (ll. 710–11):

> I eschame to thig, I can not wirk, ye wait,
> Yit wald I fane pretend to gentill stait.

As a would-be gentleman, the Fox cannot work and he is ashamed to beg. He also adds that he is of "Nature tender," and having reluctantly agreed to give up meat until Easter, he is finally granted full remission.

The Fox then walks to the river honestly bent on catching some fish: "to fang him fisch haillelie wes his intent," but when he sees the water and the stormy waves he is brought up short by the realization of what his penance would mean in actual practice. As he waits, "astonist all still in to ane stair," he notices a flock of goats under a tree, and his mood changes instantly to one of cheerfulness as he steals a little kid. The Fox has not, however, forgotten his penance (ll. 747–51):

> Syne over the heuch unto the see he hyis,
> And tuke the Kid be the hornis twane,
> And in the watter outher twyis or thryis
> He dowkit him, and till him can he sayne:
> "Ga doun, Schir Kid, cum up Schir Salmond agane!"

By this solution of his difficulties, the Fox's conscience is put to rest as he gorges himself on the "new maid Salmond."

The Fox eats his fill and lies down on his back beneath a bush, stroking his stomach in the heat of the sun. Suddenly he has another fascinating idea: "Upon this wame," he says recklessly, "set wer ane bolt full meit." A moment later, when the keeper discovers him and pins him to the ground with an arrow, the Fox is disgusted but resigned (ll. 768–71):

> "Now" (quod the Foxe), "allace and wellaway!
> Gorrit I am, and may na forther gang.
> Me think na man may speik ane word in play,
> Bot now on dayis in ernist it is tane."

He made the remark and it came true—a sort of poetic justice—and the Fox, although quite reasonably irritated by the literal humorlessness of such justice, does not think of questioning it but blames the evil times.

Henryson inherited the chief incidents of the story from earlier authors, but the character of the Fox is his own. The Fox is a consistent realist within a narrow but definite area—the area known to those who are thieves of necessity (ll. 707–9):

> ". . . how sall I leif, allace,
> Haifand nane uther craft me to defend?
> Neid causis me to steill quhair evir I wend."

Within this area, the Fox is so honest that he surprises even the Wolf, his Father Confessor. Outside of this area, prodded perhaps by his social pretensions, the Fox seems to be driven to a code of conduct that is confused and desperate, even to the manner of his death.

Why Henryson varied so widely from the traditional characterization of the Fox is a difficult question. The explanation that it was accidental seems inadequate. Perhaps the poet borrowed some of his material, as he did in other cases, from contemporary manners. If so, the key to the character of the Fox may be his marginal social status, for here is a person who speaks of himself as a thief and as one of tender nature, as one of the simple folk and as one who likes to pretend to be well-born—all in a few lines. The evidence is tantalizingly confused and contradictory, yet it does more or less describe a group of people with whom the poet might well have sympathized—the dispossessed gentry.

The dispossessed gentry had suffered the same fate as that of the peasantry who were evicted by the feudal lords, and it was the peasantry's fate, as we shall see, which the poet particularly resented. The landed gentry, especially in the highlands, had been frequently dispossessed by the reversion of lands resulting from ceaseless feuds. Caught between two cultures in a changing society, these former landowners were a confused and desperate lot, of whom Rob Roy, the later guerilla chief, was a direct descendent. Thus, this group makes an interesting parallel to Henryson's Fox: they were notorious thieves who led brief and sometimes courageous lives, and who very definitely looked down upon manual labor and up to the nobility. It would have been quite natural for the poet to be greatly interested in this group and to find qualities that he liked and disliked, as the fable indicates, in these rebellious victims of the unquiet times.

Henryson's favorite protagonist—the sturdily independent peasant —is presented in a variety of ways. In the tale of *The Lion and the Mouse,* for example, the poet's heroine, who seems to be demonstrating how a little person can stand up to a king, shares the spotlight with some of Henryson's most outspoken and specific criticism of the treasonable activities of the feudal lords. The story is simple: having captured the leader of a troup of mice who have been playing on his sleeping body, the Lion is eventually merciful and releases her; later, she returns the favor by rescuing the Lion.

The poet devotes much of the fable to the dialogue between the Lion and the Mouse in general and the various arguments of the Mouse in particular. Thus, the character of the Mouse is developed

casually in the course of the debate. When the Lion, having caught
the Mouse, asks whether she knows that he is "baith Lord and King of
beistis all," the Mouse replies with sixteen lines of persuasive reasoning. Consider "my simple povertie" and your "mychtie hie Magnyfy-
cence," she says lucidly, and note that mistakes caused by simple
negligence rather than malice and presumption should be forgiven.
So far as the mice were concerned (ll. 1440–43):

> "We wer repleit and had grit aboundance
> Of alkin thingis, sic as to us effeird;
> The sweit sesoun provokit us to dance,
> And mak sic mirth as nature to us leird."

Finally, says the Mouse, you lay so low that we thought that you were
dead.

The Lion, who is truly royal but by no means the equal of the
Mouse in an argument, falls back on the unrealistic statement that
even if he had been dead, the Mouse should have fallen to her knees
in fear. He thereupon decrees her death for the crime of treason. At
this point, the Mouse pleads guilty and throws herself upon the mercy
of the Lion. In the course of forty-one lines, she assembles a new defense with an impressive amount of learning, legal and extra-legal.
Justice should be tempered with mercy, the triumph of a lion over a
mouse would be "lytill manheid," and mouse-meat is especially un-
healthful for lions (ll. 1489–95):

> "Also it semis not your Celsitude,
> Quhilk usis daylie meittis delitious,
> To fyle your teith or lippis with my blude,
> Quhilk to your stomok is contagious;
> Unhailsum meit is of ane sarie Mous,
> And that namelie untill ane strang Lyoun,
> Wont till be fed with gentill vennesoun."

The Mouse's final argument is almost as extravagant, although it is
traditionally implied if not expressed: she may be able to return the
favor some day.

The *moralitas* of this fable, unlike that of many others, is an organic part of the story. The poet adds that the Lion is the King, who is not without the faults of "lustis, sleuth, and sleip," while the mice are the commons (ll. 1587–93):

> Thir lytill Myis ar bot the commountie,
> Wantoun, unwyse, without correctioun:
> Thair Lordis and Princis quhen that thay se
> Of Justice mak nane executioun,
> Thay dreid na thing to mak Rebellioun,
> And disobey, for quhy thay stand nane aw,
> That garris thame thair Soveranis misknaw.

Thus, Henryson is careful to explain that the common people are restless only because of the bad example set them by their lords and princes. These lords, says the poet, should consider the virtue of "pietie," or clemency, and he proceeds to make his main point (ll. 1616–18):

> I the beseik and all men for to pray
> That tressoun of this cuntrie be exyld,
> And Justice Regne, and Lordis keip thair fay
> Unto thair Soverane King, baith nycht and day.

The weight of the fable is directed against the warring feudal lords, who traffic in treason, while Henryson's sympathies remain clearly with the commons.

Although the Mouse is the heroine of the piece, Henryson does not develop her character beyond the point where she occasionally sounds like an animated roll call of arguments in behalf of the poorer citizenry. Her arguments, however, although many are based on moral and a few on mouselike grounds, are frequently both practical and legal. The result is that it is difficult to escape the impression that the poet intended the Mouse to be an educational vehicle whereby his audience could hear the arguments in favor of the peasantry.

In certain of his fables, Henryson appears to be supplying arguments to combat specific attitudes. Thus in *The Fox, the Wolf, and*

the Husbandman, the poor Husbandman answers the Wolf's pane-
gyric on loyalty with a very sensible insistence on legality of procedure. In a moment of anger, the Husbandman had sworn that the
Wolf could have his team of oxen—an oath which the Wolf and the
Fox had overheard. When the Wolf claims the team, the Husbandman, although terrified, answers him with spirit and logic (ll.
2273-79):

> "Schir" (quod the husband), "ane man may say in greif,
> And syne ganesay, fra he avise and se:
> I hecht to steill, am I thairfoir ane theif?"
> "God forbid, Schir, all hechtis suld haldin be!"
> "Gaif I my hand or oblissing" (quod he),
> "Or have ye witnes, or writ ffor to schaw?
> Schir, reif me not, but go and seik the Law!"

In this manner, the Husbandman demands that the procedure be
legal and that the Wolf produce some signature, bond, document,
or witness.

The Wolf, however, switches the argument to the subject of loyalty
as a principle (ll. 2280-86):

> "Carll" (quod the Wolff), "ane Lord, and he be leill,
> That schrinkis for schame, or doutis to be repruvit,
> His saw is ay als sickker as his Seill.
> Fy on the Leid that is not leill and lufit!
> Thy argument is fals, and eik contrufit,
> For it is said in Proverb: 'But lawte
> All uther vertewis ar nocht worth ane fle.' "

Needless to say, this praise of loyalty is not in the Bible, as the Wolf
would have the Husbandman suppose. On the other hand, whether
or not the Wolf's emphasis on the sacredness of the spoken promise,
as well as his praise of loyalty, is essentially a tribal or a feudal point
of view or both, it is clear that Henryson has the Husbandman oppose
the Wolf by insisting on correct legal procedure (ll. 2287-90):

> "Schir," said the husband, "remember of this thing:
> Ane leill man is not tane at halff ane taill.
> I may say, and ganesay, I am na King:
> Quhair is your witnes that hard I hecht thame haill?"

In effect, although the Husbandman does not question the principle that a man should be loyal, he makes the all-important point that the question of loyalty should be determined legally. A man should not be judged on half of the evidence, says the Husbandman, and the practical result of his reasoning would be to leave the question of loyalty entirely to the courts.

Unfortunately the Wolf has the Fox as a witness, and the poor Husbandman, after a trial that makes a mock of justice, is robbed and terrorized, escaping to his house only to stand and watch the door all night. In his *moralitas,* the poet says briefly that the Wolf is to be likened to a wicked man who oppresses the poor. The Husbandman represents himself, a member of the peasantry, and Henryson makes his point very clearly, showing the Husbandman fighting a one-sided and losing battle. Later in the fable the Fox observes that "God is gane to sleip" and in the same breath feigns a sympathy for the poor in order to trick the Wolf. The irony is bitter and it cuts deeply. It is clear that the poet is skeptical of the value of any appeals to the poor for loyalty.

Two of Henryson's fables appear to be devoted primarily to championing the peasantry. Plot, setting, characterization, even the poet's usually unfailing sense of humor, are subordinated in order to make his point. The *moralitas* assumes great importance, for it is the climax toward which the entire fable builds. On the other hand, the fable proper, perhaps because it does not lend itself so readily as the *moralitas* to the expression of opinion, shrinks until it becomes simply a point of departure, by way of allegory, for the poet's remarks on the contemporary scene.

Thus, the story of the *Wolf and the Lamb,* as Henryson presents it, is almost negligible: the Wolf and the Lamb are drinking from the same stream, the Wolf above the Lamb; on the incredible pretext that the Lamb is defiling the Wolf's water, the Wolf kills the Lamb. There is little or no attempt to describe the setting, although the character of the Lamb is developed briefly along the poet's favorite lines, namely, the sturdily independent peasant. Like Henryson's other heroes, the Lamb argues spiritedly in spite of his physical help-lessness, and when the ferocious Wolf falsely accuses him (ll. 2637-43),

> The selie Lamb, quaikand for verray dreid,
> On kneis fell, and said: "Schir, with your leif,
> Suppois I dar not say thairoff ye leid;
> Bot, be my Saull, I wait ye can nocht preif
> That I did ony thing that suld yow grief;
> Ye wait alswa that your accusatioun
> Failyeis ffra treuth, and contrair is to ressoun."

For the "selie" Lamb, who is quaking on his knees for very dread, to tell the Wolf that, although he would not dare to say that the Wolf is a liar, he knows nevertheless that the Wolf has no proof and that his accusation is contrary to reason and untrue—such insubordination must have seemed to Henryson's audience as revolutionary as it was futile. For the allegorical surface is never allowed to conceal the fact that the Wolf is rich and powerful and the Lamb poor and weak.

In the one-sided debate that follows, the Lamb adds learning to daring by flourishing the jargon of formal logic ("Ergo . . ."), by quoting Scripture ("halie Scripture sayis . . ."), and by citing the law ("the Law sayis . . ."). In fact, in the course of forty compelling lines, the Lamb has reduced the Wolf to a self-acknowledged monster (ll. 2693-96):

> "Na" (quod the Wolff), "thow wald Intruse ressoun,
> Quhair wrang and reif suld dwell in propertie.
> That is ane poynt, and part of fals tressoun,
> For to gar reuth remane with crueltie."

You would intrude reason where wrong and robbery should dwell, says the Wolf viciously, and to have pity abide with cruelty is treason. Thereupon he kills the Lamb. At this point, Henryson has done everything in his power to show that the Wolf is wrong and the Lamb right: his characterization is simple and unambiguous. With the rhetorical question, "Wes not this reuth?" the poet goes on to the *moralitas* and what is clearly his main objective.

The Lamb, says Henryson, signifies poor people, including all peasants, to whom life is half a purgatory as they attempt by loyalty to earn a suitable livelihood. There are three types of Wolves, the poet says: Lawyers, Mighty Men, and Men of Inheritance; and he proceeds to describe and comment upon the methods of each in a manner which leaves no doubt as to his true attitude. The Lawyer perverts the law. He mingles.falsehood with polished terms, pretending that all that he shows is "Gospell," but for a bribe he over--throws the poor man, smothering the right and causing the wrong to win out. Although the poet is aware of exactly how corrupt the law has become, he apparently has lost neither his faith in it nor his capacity for sustained indignation at its abuse. Here he comments (ll. 2721–27):

> O man of Law! let be thy subteltie,
> With nice gimpis, and fraudis Intricait,
> And think that God in his Divinitie
> The wrang, the richt, of all thy werkis wait:
> For prayer, price, for hie nor law estait,
> Of fals querrellis se thow mak na defence;
> Hald with the richt, hurt not thy conscience.

Hell's fire, the poet adds, shall be the reward of such Wolves.

Mighty Men have great plenty but are so greedy and covetous that they will not allow the poor man to live in peace. Although the poor man and his family will starve to death, these Mighty Men take his farm away from him. The poet's comment on this type of Wolf is bitterly resentful (ll. 2735–41):

> O man! but mercie, quhat is in thy thocht,
> War than ane Wolf, and thow culd understand?
> Thow hes aneuch; the pure husband richt nocht
> Bot croip and caff upon ane clout of land.
> For Goddis aw, how durst thow tak on hand,
> And thow in Barn and Byre sa bene, and big,
> To put him fra his tak and gar him thig?

For fear of God, says the poet, how dare you evict a man from his holding and make him beg?

Henryson comments upon Men of Inheritance with considerable fire and fury (ll. 2756–62):

> Hes thow not reuth to gar thy tennentis sweit
> In to thy laubour with faynt and hungrie wame,
> And syne hes lytill gude to drink or eit,
> With his menye at evin quhen he cummis hame?
> Thow suld dreid for rychteous Goddis blame;
> For it cryis ane vengeance unto the hevinnis hie,
> To gar ane pure man wirk but Meit or fe.

It cries a vengeance to the high heavens, says the poet with Carlylesque vehemence, to make a poor man work without meat or fee. Thou shouldst fear the righteous wrath of God!

It becomes increasingly evident that Henryson not only champions the poor but also specifically identifies himself with the poor. The conjecture that the poet was not a court poet would gain convincing support from this internal evidence if from nothing else. In the fable of *The Sheep and the Dog,* for example, Henryson speaks in the first person of "we poor people" and expands the moral into a direct, personal plea for the poor.

One of the poet's aims in *The Sheep and the Dog* is to criticize both the ecclesiastical and the civil courts—an objective which he admirably accomplishes. At the same time, it is clear that Henryson is building in the course of the fable toward his personal comment in the *moralitas.* As the fable begins, a Dog hales a Sheep into court simply "because that he wes pure." The Sheep is so frightened by the illegal force and talent arrayed against him that he "durst lay na mouth on eird" until he has appeared before the awful judge.

Despite his well-founded fear, the Sheep is so stung by the unjust charge and the flagrantly lawless procedure that he delivers his one and only answer with great spirit. Twice Henryson makes the point that the Sheep is carrying on among many legal complexities without a lawyer—an indication perhaps of the poet's faith in the staying power of the people whom the Sheep symbolizes, and a possible clue to the audience for which he was writing. Finally, in spite of the fact that the court is "corruptit all ffor meid, aganis gude faith, Law, and eik conscience," the fact that the Sheep is a "selie Innocent," and the fact that the decision against him is a "wrangous Jugement," the Sheep is nevertheless convicted, pays his fine by selling the wool off of his back, and returns to the field naked and bare. Henryson makes the tragic conclusion as inevitable as it is swift, and as unjust as it is inevitable.

In the *moralitas,* the poet states at once that the Sheep personifies the poor commons who are oppressed daily by tyrannical men, while the Wolf and his assistants stand for various corrupt court-officials, whose crimes he describes. At this point, however, Henryson departs from his usual treatment and announces that he himself happened to pass by the place where the Sheep lay and heard the Sheep's lamentation (ll. 1286–90):

> "Allace" (quod he), "this cursit Consistorie,
> In middis of the winter now is maid,
> Quhen Boreas with blastis bitterlie
> And hard froistes thir flouris doun can faid;
> On bankis bair now may I mak na baid."

(The poet's very effective use of the winter season to set the tone of the Sheep's lamentation is characteristic.) As he creeps into a hollow, shivering with the cold, the Sheep casts his eyes unto the heavens high and addresses his Maker in no uncertain terms (ll. 1295–98):

> . . . "Lord God, quhy sleipis thow sa lang?
> Walk, and discerne my cause, groundit on richt;
> Se how I am, be fraud, maistrie, and slicht,
> Peillit full bair."

This Job-like plea to God, with its intimacy, moral conviction, and definite trace of irritation, has the force and flavor of a sermon by an old Scots preacher.

Henryson is not satisfied with the Sheep's plea alone, for the poet himself continues in the same vein (ll. 1298–1306):

> . . . and so is mony one
> Now in this warld, richt wonder, wo begone!
>
> Se how this cursit sone of covetice,
> Loist hes baith lawtie and eik Law.
> Now few or nane will execute Justice,
> In falt of quhome the pure man is overthraw.
> The veritie, suppois the Juge it knaw,
> He is so blindit with affectioun,
> But dreid, for micht, he lettis the richt go doun.

In the light of the poet's knowledge of and faith in the legal process, this condemnation of the custodians of the law takes on added weight. It should be noted, however, that the poet tends to blame it on the sin of covetousness. Henryson then makes his own personal plea to God, placing the blame squarely upon the feudal laird (ll. 1307–13):

> Seis thow not (Lord) this warld overturnit is,
> As quha wald change gude gold in leid or tyn;
> The pure is peillit, the Lord [Laird] may do na mis;
> And Simonie is haldin for na syn.
> Now is he blyith with okker maist may wyn;
> Gentrice is slane, and pietie is ago,
> Allace (gude Lord) quhy thoilis thow it so?

In this and the preceding passage, the poet reaches the heights of his criticism of the age. Simony (he says) is held for no sin, and now he is blithe who may gain the most with usury; honorable feeling is slain and pity is gone; the poor are plundered and the laird may do no wrong.

These passages are perhaps the key to Henryson's attitude toward his times. In selecting the "cursed sin of covetousness" in general and usury in particular, the poet is echoing the continual cry of the church long before and after Henryson's day in its tardy adjustment to a developing money economy. By referring to "gentrice" and "pietie," the poet is emphasizing those qualities which the feudal lord should possess in order to make the *status quo* run more smoothly, while the charge of simony was a stock criticism of the church in Henryson's time. All of these criticisms are passionately felt but they are also fairly conventional and typical of the times. The novelty of the poet's comment lies in the fact that he selects the feudal lords rather than any other group as the chief culprits.

In the concluding stanza, Henryson turns sadly to prayer, and it is clear that the poet, as a devout Catholic, feels that this is the only avenue of appeal open to the poor (ll. 1314-20):

> Thow tholis this evin for our grit offence,
> Thow sendis us troubill, and plaigis soir,
> As hunger, derth, grit weir, or Pestilence;
> Bot few amendis now thair lyfe thairfoir.
> We pure pepill as now may do no moir
> Bot pray to the, sen that we ar opprest
> In to this eirth, grant us in hevin gude rest.

Thou sendeth us trouble and sore plagues (says the poet) such as hunger, dearth, great war, or pestilence . . . We poor people at this time may do no more than pray to thee; since we are oppressed on this earth, grant us good rest in heaven. Thus, Henryson's ultimate solution of the problems of his day, above and beyond his particular aversion toward the feudal lords and his compassion for the poor, is probably the same as that of any other intelligent man of good will in his age. It would be ridiculous to expect the poet to be anything else than the product, although an outstanding one, of his own times—

times when, due in part to the fact that he lived in a culture steeped in the concept of original sin, no one would readily think of taking direct action to change a world which God had seen fit so to create.

Henryson's championship of the peasantry and his criticism of the feudal lords are two sides of the same coin. It should not be thought that the poet's attitude toward the poor is found only in the *Fables,* for the same note is struck in his minor poems, especially in his *Want of Wyse Men* where he declares that the poor "ar all opprest" and that flatterers "pike and pill" the poor, and in his *Prayer for the Pest* where he identifies himself once more with the poor, praying God to have mercy "of us, indigent and peure." Nor should it be thought, on the other hand, that the poet's attitude toward the poor was common in his day. In the prologue to the *Fables,* Henryson says that his "author" would not make light of "hie nor low estate," and one can readily understand why an author would not care to antagonize the predatory nobles. The statement that he will not make light of low estate, however, plus the fact that he more than carries out his promise, makes Henryson's verse virtually unique in fifteenth-century literature.

The only parallel to Henryson in English literature is the author of *Piers Plowman,* who is critical equally of church and state, of the nobility, townsfolk, and peasantry. The author of *Piers,* however, treats the demands of the peasants for a rise in the standard of living as evidence of laziness and vagabondage. Henryson never accuses the peasantry of anything worse than justifiably following the bad example of the feudal lords, while his usual attitude, as we have seen, is explicitly to favor the poor. For the poet not only champions the peasantry and identifies himself with the poor, but also assembles a series of significantly *practical* arguments in support of his point of view—a fact which offers another clue to Henryson's occupation and even the audience for which he is writing. At heart, although both would return to an idealized *status quo,* the author of *Piers* is a conformist, writing from a clerical point of view, whereas Henryson is an individualist writing from a humanitarian point of view.

The problem of Henryson's audience is perhaps insoluble. He writes for anyone who wants to read, no doubt, but he is not a court poet—a fact which at once limits his possible audience and sets him apart from the other Scottish Chaucerians. Although the dialect of Middle Scots was never spoken, Henryson's verses, read aloud, would probably have been easily understood by his contemporaries at any social level and, as a schoolteacher, the poet's most obvious audience would have been in his own classroom, a group which could have included the children of the townsfolk, the gentry, and a few perhaps of the peasantry and nobility. Such a conjecture would help explain the pedagogical device of the Aesopic fable as a vehicle for the defense of the peasantry and the criticism of their oppressors.

Henryson was writing, as I have suggested, in a violent age of transition from a feudal to a mercantile economy. As we now see it, the change was inescapable, and the poet, unlike the predatory feudal lords who were paradoxically hastening the decline of feudalism by forcibly dispossessing the peasantry, is passionately condemning the clear and manifold injustices which were an inevitable part of this transition. If asked for his solution to the injustices against which he inveighs, Henryson would doubtless have recommended a return to a more consistent feudalism, although feudalism never actually functioned smoothly and inevitably bred the seeds of its own destruction. Henryson, like Chaucer, is a poet of the Middle Ages. Yet, unlike Chaucer, Henryson is unique among British poets in this respect that, in a literary age devoted to the imitation of foreign models, in an age when poets mentioned the peasantry, if at all, with unquestioned disdain, in an age when the cause of the peasant was not only unheard of but also virtually inconceivable, Henryson speaks out boldly for the poor. In any age, the poet would have been a humanitarian of outstanding insight, integrity, and compassion.

APPENDIX A

Note: W. A. Geddie's *Bibliography of Middle Scots Poets* (1912) is complete to the year 1910. The *Cambridge Bibliography of English Literature* (1941) has several omissions.

I. MANUSCRIPTS

S. J.* St. John's College, Cambridge; a MS of the *Testament,* in a sixteenth-century hand (cf. H. H. Wood, ed., *The Poems and Fables of Robert Henryson,* p. xxvi), following a fifteenth-century copy of Chaucer's *Troilus and Criseyde.*

Kinaston.* Sir Francis Kinaston's MS Latin translation of Chaucer's *Troilus and Criseyde* and Henryson's *Testament of Cresseid,* accompanied by an emended version of Thynne's printed text. [Bodleian MS, Add. C. 287, c. 1640.]

II. PRINTED TEXTS

William Thynne, ed. The Workes of Geffray Chaucer. London, 1532.* 2d ed., 1542.* Reprinted, c. 1545. (*Testament,* fol. cc *verso*–ccv *verso.*) [In the edition c. 1545, as in the earlier editions, the *Testament* follows the fifth book of the *Troilus and Criseyde* and is introduced with the following words: "Thus endeth the fyfth booke, and laste of Troylus: and here foloweth the pyteful and dolorous testament of fayre Creseyde." No mention of Henryson's authorship is made.]

John Stow, ed. The Woorkes of Geffrey Chaucer. London, 1561. (*Testament,* fol. cxciv–cxcvii.) [A reprint of Thynne with additions.]

Henry Charteris, printer. The Testament of Cresseid. Edinburgh, 1593.* (*British Museum,* C. 21, c. 14.) [The best text, cf. H. H. Wood, ed., *Poems and Fables of . . . Henryson,* p. xxv.]

Thomas Speght, ed. The Workes of our Antient and lerned English

* Unavailable to present writer.

Poet, Geffrey Chaucer. London, 1598. 2d ed., 1602.* (*Testament,* fol. 194–197.) [A reprint of Thynne with alterations.]

The Testament of Cresseid. Glasgow [?], 1663.* [Trinity College; Cambridge: xv, a, 55.]

John Urry, ed. The Works of Geoffrey Chaucer. London, 1721. (*Testament,* pp. 333–38.) [A reprint of Thynne. For the first time in editions of Chaucer, Henryson is here named the author of the *Testament.*]

John Bell, ed. The Poets of Great Britain. 109 vols. London, 1776–1803. (*Testament,* X [1782], 5–27.)

Robert Anderson, ed. The Works of the British Poets. 13 vols. London, 1795. (*Testament,* I, 409–14.)

James Sibbald, ed. Chronicle of Scottish Poetry. 4 vols. Edinburgh, 1802. (*Testament,* I, 157–76.)

Alexander Chalmers, ed. The Works of the English Poets. 21 vols. London, 1810. (*Testament,* I, 294–99.) [No mention of Henryson's authorship.]

George Chalmers, ed. Robene and Makyne, and the Testament of Cresseid. Edinburgh, 1824.* [Charteris text. See Geddie, *Bibliography,* p. 172.]

David Laing, ed. The Poems and Fables of Robert Henryson. Edinburgh, 1865. [The first collected edition.]

J. Ross, ed. The Book of Scottish Poems. Edinburgh, 1878. (Henryson's poems, including the *Testament,* I, 131–70.) [Laing's text, partly modernized. *Testament* ascribed to Johnstoun. See Geddie, *Bibliography,* pp. 10, 173.]

H. M. Fitzgibbon, ed. Early English Poetry. London, 1887.* (*Testament,* in part, and other poems by Henryson, pp. 47–61.) [Modernized extracts.]

George Eyre-Todd, ed. Mediaeval Scottish Poetry. Glasgow, 1892. (*Testament,* pp. 103–25.) [Laing's text.]

W. W. Skeat. Chaucerian and other Pieces. Oxford, 1897. (*Testament,* pp. 327–46.) [Charteris text, collated with Thynne in footnotes.]

Edward Arber, ed. Selections from the English Poets. The Dunbar Anthology. London, 1901. (*Testament,* pp. 156–78.) [Modernized.]

G. Gregory Smith, ed. The Poems of Robert Henryson. 3 vols. Edinburgh, Scottish Text Society, 1906–14. [Texts from Charteris, Thynne, and Kinaston MS *in extenso.*]

George Douglas. The Book of Scottish Poetry. London, 1910.* (*Testament and Robene and Makyne,* pp. 73–99.) [See Geddie, *Bibliography,* pp. 12, 174.]

W. A. Neilson and K. G. T. Webster, eds. Chief British Poets of the Fourteenth and Fifteenth Centuries. New York, 1916. (*Testament,* pp. 367–75.) [Charteris text with brief but excellent comment.]

W. M. Metcalfe, ed. The Poems of Robert Henryson. London, 1917. [An abridged repetition of Laing.]

Bruce Dickins, ed. The Testament of Cresseid. Edinburgh, 1925. [The first modern separate printing. Charteris text, emended.]

A. Attwater, ed. Henryson: The Testament of Cresseid. "Cambridge Plain Texts." Cambridge [England], 1926. [No editorial comment.]

H. M. R. Murray, ed. Selected Fables, The Testament of Cresseid, and Robene and Makyne. London, 1930.

H. H. Wood, ed. The Poems and Fables of Robert Henryson. Edinburgh. 1933. [The most recent scholarly edition.]

R. K. Gordon, ed. The Story of Troilus. London, 1934. (*Testament,* pp. 351–67.)

M. M. Gray, ed. Scottish Poetry from Barbour to James VI. London, 1935. (*Testament,* pp. 58–75.)

Hugh MacDiarmid (pseud.), ed. The Golden Treasury of Scottish Poetry. New York, 1941. (*Testament,* pp. 194–215.)

APPENDIX B

PRECEDENTS FOR HENRYSON'S FOUR HORSES OF THE SUN

OVIDIAN

Ovid
Pyroeis, Eous, Aethon, Phlegon

Pseudo-Bede (in part)
Eous . . . oriens vel surgens
Aethon . . . elatus
Pyrois . . . igneus
Phlegon . . . acclivis

Lactantius Placidus
Pyrois, Eous, Aethon, ac Phlegon

Ovide Moralisé
Pirouz . . . rouges . . . fu
Eoüz . . . blanc
Ethon . . . resplent la colour
Phlegon . . . grant chalour

Berchorius
Aethon . . . rubeus
Eous . . . splendens
Pyrois . . . ardens
Phlegon . . . urens terram

Froissart
Pirrous . . . rouge
Eöus . . . blans com neje
Ethon
Phlegron . . . calour

FULGENTIAN

Fulgentius
Erythreus . . . rubeus . . . matutino
Actaeon . . . splendens . . . tertiae horae
Lampos . . . ardens . . . umbilicum diei
Philogeus . . . terram amans . . .
hora nona

Pseudo-Bede (in part)
Erythros . . . rubeus . . . mane
Acteon . . . splendens . . . circa
tertiam
Lampon . . . ardens . . . meridie
Philoges . . . amans terram . . .
occidendo

Bede
Erytheus . . . rubeus
Acteus . . . splendens
Lampas . . . ardens
Philogeus . . . amans terram

Myth. Vat. I
Erythraeus . . . rubeus . . . matu-
tino
Aethon . . . splendens
Lampus . . . ardens

OVIDIAN

FULGENTIAN

Lydgate
Pirous so rede
Pirrous . . . up drawe
Flegonte

Chaucer
Pirous

Philogeus . . . terram amans . . .
vespere

Myth. Vat. II
Erythraeus . . . rubeus . . . matutino
Aethon . . . splendens . . . tertia
hora
Lampus . . . ardens . . . sum-
mum diei
Philogeus . . . terrae amans . . .
nona hora

Myth. Vat. III
Erythraeus . . . rubens . . . mane
Aethon . . . splendens . . . hora
tertia
Lampos . . . lucens vel ardens . . .
die media
Philogeus . . . amans terram . . .
occidendo

Gower
Eritheüs . . . hote . . . red
Acteos the bryhte
Lampes
Philogeüs

SELECTED BIBLIOGRAPHY

Aeneas Sylvius. See Pii Secundi.

Al-Andalusī. See Nykl.

Albohazen ('Alí ibn Abí al-Rajjál, Abú al Hasen, al Kurtub al-Shaibání). Liber de Fatis Astrorum. Venice, 1485. In the Sterling Memorial Library at Yale University.

Albumasar (Ja 'Far ibn Muhammad Al-Balkhi). Introductorium in Astronomian. Venice, 1489. In the New York Public Library.

Alchabitus ('Abd al Azziz ibn 'Uthman al Kabisi). Libellus Ysagogicus. Venice, 1485. In the Columbia University Library.

Ambrosi, L. La Psicologia della Immaginazione nella storia filosofia. Rome, 1898.

Andreas Capellanus. See Parry.

Andrews, W. Bygone Church Life in Scotland. London, 1899.

Babington, Churchill, ed. The Repressor of Over Much Blaming of the Clergy, by Reginald Pecock. 2 vols. London, 1860.

Bacon, Roger. See Bridges.

Bale, J. Illustrium Maioris Britanniae Scriptorum. Ipswich, 1548.

Bartholomaeus Anglicus. De Proprietatibus Rerum. Tr. by John de Trevisa. London, 1535.

Bede. See Giles.

Bellesheim, A. History of the Catholic Church of Scotland. 4 vols. London, 1887–90.

Benoît de Sainte-Maure. See Constans.

Berchorius (Bersuire). Opera Omnia. Agrippina Coloniae, 1712.

Bergen, Henry, ed. Lydgate's Fall of Princes. 4 vols. Washington [D.C.], The Carnegie Institute of Washington, 1923–27.

—— Lydgate's Troy Book. 4 vols. London, Early English Text Society, 1906–35.

Betussi, G., ed. Della Genealogia de gli dei di M. Giovanni Boccaccio. Venice, 1627.

Beveridge, Erskine. A Bibliography of Works Relating to Dunfermline. Dunfermline, 1901.

—— The Burgh Records of Dunfermline. Edinburgh, 1917.

Bezold, Friedrich von. Das Fortleben der antiken Götter im mittelalter-lichen Humanismus. Leipzig, 1922.

Boccaccio. *See* Betussi; Griffin; Moutier; Myrick.

Bode, G. H., ed. Scriptores Rerum Mythicarum Latini Tres. Cellis, 1834.

Boer, Cornelis de. Ovide Moralisé. 5 vols. Koninklijke Academie, Vols. XV, XXI, XXX, No. 3, XXXVII, XLIII. Amsterdam, 1915–38.

Boll, Franz. "Die Lebensalter ein Beitrag zur antiken Ethologie und zur Geschichte der Zahlen," *Neue Jahrbücher für das klassische altertum Geschichte und deutsche Literatur,* XXXI (1913), 89–145.

Bouche-Leclercq, Auguste. L'Astrologie grecque. Paris, 1899.

Brett, G. S. A History of Psychology. 3 vols. London, 1912–21.

Bridges, J. H. The Opus Majus of Roger Bacon. 3 vols. London, 1900.

Brown, J. T. T. The Authorship of the Kingis Quair. Glasgow, 1896.

Brown, P. H. Early Travellers in Scotland. Edinburgh, 1891.

—— History of Scotland. 3 vols. Cambridge, 1900–1909.

—— Scotland before 1700 from Contemporary Documents. Edinburgh, 1893.

Buchan, John. A History of English Literature. New York, 1929.

Buckner, J. C. R. Clark's Guide to Dunfermline. Dunfermline, 1890.

Bullett, Gerald. "The Fortunes of Cressida," *New Statesman,* XXI (1923), 361–63.

Bundy, M. W. The Theory of Imagination in Classical and Mediaeval Thought, "University of Illinois Studies in Language and Literature," XII, 2–3. Urbana, 1927.

Bunte, B. Hygini astronomica. Leipzig, 1875.

Burton, J. H. *The Scot Abroad.* Edinburgh, 1883.

Bush, Douglas. Mythology and the Renaissance Tradition in English Poetry. Minneapolis, 1932.

Caird, James B. "Some Reflections on Scottish Literature," *Scottish Periodical,* I (Summer, 1947), 6–24.

Calendar of Letters, Despatches, and State Papers . . . between England and Spain . . . 1485–1509. Ed. G. A. Bergenroth. London, 1862.

Cameron, A. I. The Apostolic Camera and Scottish Benefices. London, 1934.

Chadwick, Dorothy. Social Life in the Days of Piers Plowman. "Cambridge Studies in Medieval Life and Thought." New York, 1922.

Chambers, Robert. Domestic Annals of Scotland. 2 vols. Edinburgh, 1858.

Charteris, Henry (printer). The Testament of Cresseid. Edinburgh, 1593. (British Museum, C. 21, c. 14.)

Cholmeley, H. P., ed. John of Gaddesden and the Rosa Medicinae. Oxford, 1912.

Clay, R. M. The Mediaeval Hospitals of England. London, 1909.

Cochran-Patrick, R. W. Mediaeval Scotland. Glasgow, 1892.

Constans, Léopold, ed. Le Roman de Troie par Benoît de Sainte-Maure. 6 vols. Paris, 1904–12.

Cooke, J. D. "Euhemerism: a Mediaeval Interpretation of Classical Paganism," *Speculum,* II (1927), 396–410.

Coulter, C. C. "The Genealogy of the Gods," *Vassar Mediaeval Studies* (New Haven, 1923), pp. 317–41.

Coulton, G. G. Medieval Panorama. Cambridge, 1939.

—— Scottish Abbeys and Social Life. Cambridge, 1933.

Cowan, Samuel. The Royal House of Stuart. 2 vols. London, 1908.

Cumont, Franz. "La Théologie solaire du paganisme romain," *in* Académie des Inscriptions et Belles-Lettres, Paris. *Mémoires présentés par divers savants,* XII (1913), 447–79.

Curry, W. C. Chaucer and the Mediaeval Sciences. New York, 1926.

Dante. Opere di Dante Alighieri. Ed. E. Moore. Oxford, 1924.

Dick, A., ed. Martiani Capellae De Nuptiis Philologiae et Mercurii. Leipzig, 1925.

Diebler, A. R. Henrisone's Fabeldichtungen. Halle, 1885.

—— "Henrisone's Fabeln," *Anglia,* IX (1886), 337–90.

Dodd, W. G. Courtly Love in Chaucer and Gower. Boston, 1913. (Harvard Studies.)

Douglas, Gawin. See Small.

Dowden, John. The Medieval Church in Scotland. Glasgow, 1910.

Dreyer, J. L. E. "Mediaeval Astronomy," *Studies in the History and Method of Science.* Ed. C. J. Singer (1921), II, 106–20.

Duhem, Pierre. Le Système du monde: histoire des doctrines cosmologiques de Platon à Copernic. 4 vols. Paris, 1913–17.

Dunbar, William. See Small.

Erdmann, A., ed. *Lydgate's Siege of Thebes.* London, Early English Text Society, 1911.

Eyre-Todd, George. Mediaeval Scottish Poetry. Glasgow, 1892.

Eyssenhardt, F. R. Macrobius. Leipzig, 1868.

Fansler, D. S. Chaucer and the Roman de la Rose. New York, 1914.

Farmer, H. G. *A History of Music in Scotland.* London, n.d. [1947?].

Fassbinder, Franz. Das Leben und die Werke des Benediktiners Pierre Berçuire. Bonn, 1917.

Ferraz, Marin. De la Psychologie de Saint Augustin. Paris, 1862.

Festa, Nicola, ed. Francesco Petrarca L'Africa. Florence, 1926.

Firmicus. See Kroll and Skutsch; Pruckner.

Frey-Sallmann, Alma. Aus dem Nachleben antiker Gottergestalten. Leipzig, 1931.

Froissart. The Chronicle of Froissart. Tr. by Lord Berners, introd. W. P. Ker. London, 1902.

—— Œuvres de Froissart. Ed. A. Scheler. 3 vols. Brussels, 1870–72.

Fuchs, B. A. Die Ikonographie der 7 Planeten in der Kunst italiens bis zum Ausgang des Mittelalters. Munich, 1909.

Fulgentius. See Liebeschütz; Staveren.

Geddie, W. A Bibliography of Middle Scots Poets. London, Scottish Text Society, 1912.

Gest Hystoriale. See Panton.

Giles, J. A., ed. and tr. The Complete Works of Venerable Bede. 12 vols. London, 1843–44.

Godwin, W. W. Plutarch's Morals. Boston, 1870.

Godwin, William. Life of Geoffrey Chaucer, the Early English Poet. 2 vols. London, 1803.

Golding, L. "The Scottish Chaucerians," Saturday Review, CXXXIV (November 25, 1922), 782–83.

Gordon, R. K. The Story of Troilus. London, 1934.

Gower, John. See Macaulay.

Grant, I. F. Everyday Life in Old Scotland. London, 1931–32.

—— The Social and Economic Development of Scotland before 1603. Edinburgh, 1930.

Gray, M. M. Scottish Poetry from Barbour to James VI. London, 1935.

Grierson, H. J. C. The Modern Scot. London, 1934.

Griffin, N. E., ed. Guido de Columnis Historia Destructionis Troiae. Cambridge, Mediaeval Academy of America, 1936.

—— and A. B. Myrick, eds. The Filostrato of Giovanni Boccaccio. London, 1929.

Grimm, F. M. Astronomical Lore in Chaucer. Lincoln, 1919.

Gruppe, Otto. Geschichte der klassischen Mythologie. Leipzig, 1921.

Hailes, Lord (Sir David Dalrymple). Ancient Scottish Poems. Edinburgh, 1770.

Hammond, W. A., ed. and tr. Aristotle's Psychology. London, 1902.

Hartridge, R. A. R. A History of Vicarages in the Middle Ages. Cambridge, 1930.

Haskins, C. H. "The Reception of Arabic Science in England," *English Historical Review,* XXX (1915), 57–69.

Haynes, F., "Shakespeare and the Troy Story," *Howard College Bulletin* LXXX (1922), 67–131.

Henderson, Ebenezer, ed., The Annals of Dunfermline. Glasgow, 1879.

Henderson, T. F. Scottish Vernacular Literature. London, 1898.

Henley, W. E. "Robert Henryson," *The English Poets,* ed. T. H. Ward. 5 vols. London, 1880–1918, I, 137–39.

Henryson. *See* Charteris, Laing, Metcalfe, H. M. R. Murray, G. G. Smith, H. H. Wood, and Appendix A.

Hibbard, L. A. Mediaeval Romance in England. New York, 1924.

Huizinga, Johan. The Waning of the Middle Ages. Trans. F. Hopman. London, 1924.

Hunt, U. D. Le Sommaire en prose des Metamorphoses d'Ovide. Paris, 1925.

Huxley, Aldous. Essays New and Old. New York, 1927.

Hyginus. *See* Bunte; Staveren.

Innes, Cosmo. Scotland in the Middle Ages. Edinburgh, 1860.

—— Sketches of Early Scotch History and Social Progress. Edinburgh, 1861.

James I. *See* Lawson; Skeat.

John, L. C. The Elizabethan Sonnet Sequences. New York, 1938.

Jones, C. W., "A Note on Concepts of the Inferior Planets in the Early Middle Ages," *Isis,* XXIV (1936), 397–99.

Jones, W. P., "A Source for Henryson's *Robene and Makyne?*" *Modern Language Notes,* XLVI (November, 1931), 457–58.

Jourdain, Amable. Recherches critiques sur l'âge et l'origine des traductions latines d'Aristote. Paris, 1843.

Ker, W. P. Form and Style in Poetry. London, 1929.

Kirby, T. A. Chaucer's Troilus, a Study in Courtly Love. "Louisiana State University Studies," No. 39. University [La.], 1940.

Krapp, G. P. Troilus and Cressida. New York, 1932.

Kreitz, Erwin. Die Tiere in den Hauptwerken der älteren schottischen Literatur. Halle-Wittenberg, 1932.

Kroll, Wilhelm. Die Kosmologie des Plinius. Breslau, 1930.

Kroll, Wilhelm and F. Skutsch, eds. Iulii Firmici Materni Matheseos Libri VIII. 2 vols. Leipzig, 1897–1913.

Lactantius Placidus. *See* Staveren.

Laing, David, ed. The Poems and Fables of Robert Henryson. Edinburgh, 1865.

——— The Poetical Works of Sir David Lyndsay. 3 vols. Edinburgh, 1879.

Langlois, Ernest, ed. Le Roman de la Rose. 5 vols. Paris, 1914–24.

Laud Troy Book. *See* Wülfing.

Lawson, A., ed. The Kingis Quair and The Quare of Jelusy. London, 1910.

Legrand, Louis. La Notion philosophique de la trinité chez Saint Augustin. Paris, 1930.

Leland, John. Commentarii de scriptoribus Britannicis. Oxford, 1709.

Lewis, C. S. The Allegory of Love. Oxford, 1936.

Leyden, John, ed. The Complaynt of Scotland. Edinburgh, 1801.

Liebeschütz, Hans, ed. Fulgentius Metaforalis. Leipzig, 1926.

Lilly, William. Christian Astrology. London, 1647.

Loomis, R. S. "Chaucer's Eight Year Sickness," *Modern Language Notes,* LIX (March, 1944), 178–80.

Lounsbury, T. R. Studies in Chaucer. 3 vols. New York, 1892.

Lowell, J. R. The English Poets. London, 1888.

Lydgate, John. *See* Bergen; Erdmann; MacCracken; Schick; Sieper; Steele; Triggs.

Lyndsay, David. *See* Laing.

Macaulay, G. C., ed. The Complete Works of John Gower. 4 vols. Oxford, 1899–1902.

MacCracken, H. N., ed. The Minor Poems of John Lydgate. 2 vols. London, Early English Text Society, 1911–34.

——— Studies in the Life and Writings of John Lydgate. Unpublished Harvard thesis, 1907.

MacDiarmid, Hugh (pseud.), ed. The Golden Treasury of Scottish Poetry. New York, 1941.

Mackay, Æ. J. G., ed. The Historie and Cronicles of Scotland . . . by Robert Lindesay of Pitscottie. 3 vols. London, Scottish Text Society, 1899–1911.

Mackenzie, A. M. An Historical Survey of Scottish Literature to 1714. London, 1933.

——— The Rise of the Stewarts. London, 1935.

Macrobius. *See* Eyssenhardt.

Major. A History of Greater Britain by John Major. Tr. by A. Constable. Edinburgh, Scottish Historical Society, 1892.

Manilius. *See* Wageningen; Pruckner.

Manley, J. M. Some New Light on Chaucer. New York, 1926.

Martianus Capella. *See* Dick.

Metcalfe, W. M. The Poems of Robert Henryson. London, 1917.

Migne, J. P., ed. Patrologiae Cursus Completus: Patrologia Latina. 221 vols. Paris, 1844–64.

Millar, J. H. A Literary History of Scotland. New York, 1903.

Moffatt, J. The Bible in Scots Literature. London, 1924.

Moore, Marianne. "Feeling and Precision," *Sewanee Review,* LII (Autumn, 1944), 499–507.

Moryson, Fynes. An Itinerary Containing His Ten Yeares Travell. 4 vols. Glasgow, 1908.

Moutier, Ignazio, ed. Opere volgari di Giovanni Boccaccio. 7 vols. Florence, 1827–34.

Murison, William. Sir David Lyndsay, Poet, and Satirist of the Old Church in Scotland. Cambridge, 1938.

Murray, H. M. R., ed. Selected Fables, The Testament of Cresseid and Robene and Makyne. London, 1930.

Murray, J. A. H., ed. The Complaynt of Scotland. London, Early English Text Society, 1872–73.

Neckham, Alexander. *See* Wright.

Neilson, W. A. The Origins and Sources of the Court of Love. *Harvard Studies and Notes in Philology and Literature,* Vol. VI, Boston, 1899.

—— and K. G. T. Webster, eds. Chief British Poets of the Fourteenth and Fifteenth Centuries. New York, 1916.

Nykl, A. R., ed. and tr. A Book containing the Risāla known as *The Dove's Neck-Ring* about Love and Lovers (Abū Muhammed 'Ali ibn Hazm Al-Andalusi). Paris, 1931.

Ovide Moralisé. *See* Boer.

Owst, G. R. Literature and Pulpit in Medieval England. Cambridge, 1933.

—— Preaching in Medieval England, Cambridge, 1926.

Panofsky, Erwin. Studies in Iconology. "Bryn Mawr College. Mary Flexner Lectures on the Humanities," No. 7. New York, 1939.

Panton, G. A., and D. Donaldson, eds. The "Gest Hystoriale" of the Destruction of Troy. London, Early English Text Society, 1874.

Parr, Johnstone. "Cresseid's Leprosy Again," *Modern Language Notes,* LX (November, 1945), 487–91.

Parry, J. J., ed. and tr. The Art of Courtly Love by Andreas Capellanus. New York, 1941.

Patch, H. R. The Goddess Fortuna in Mediaeval Literature. Cambridge, 1927.

Pecock. *See* Babington.

Pedro de Ayala. *See* Calendar.

Perrow, E. C. "The Last Will and Testament as a Form of Literature," *Transactions of the Wisconsin Academy of Science,* XVII (1914), 682–753.

Petrarch. *See* Festa.

Pii Secundi, Pontificis Max. Commentarii Rerum Memorabilium, quae temporibus suis contigerunt. Frankfort, 1614.

Pinkerton, John, ed. *Ancient Scotish Poems.* London, 1786.

Pitscottie. *See* Mackay.

Plessow, Max. Geschichte der Fabeldichtung in England bis zu John Gay. Berlin, 1906.

Pliny. Natural History. Ed. H. Rackham. London, 1938–40.

Power, E. E. Medieval English Nunneries c. 1275 to 1535. "Cambridge Studies in Medieval Life and Thought." Cambridge, 1922.

—— Medieval People. London, 1924.

Power, William. Literature and Oatmeal. "Voice of Scotland Series," No. 3. London, 1935.

Pruckner, N., ed. Iulii Firmici Materni . . . Astronomicon Lib. VIII per Nicolaum Prucknerum . . . his accesserunt Claudii Ptolemaei . . . Quadripartitum . . . Hermetis . . . Centum Aphoris . . . Bethem Centiloquium . . . De Horis Planetarum . . . Almansoris . . . Propositiones . . . Zahelis . . . De Electionibus . . . Messahalah De Ratione Circuli & Stellarum . . . Omar De Nativitatibus . . . Manilii . . . Astronomicon . . . Othonis Brunfelsii De Diffinitionibus . . . Basle, 1533.

Pseudo-Bede. De Mundi Coelestis Terrestrisque Constitutione Liber, ed. J. P. Migne, *Patrologia Latina.* Paris, 1844–64, XC, 881–910.

Ptolemy. *See* Pruckner.

Quiller-Couch, Sir Arthur. Studies in Literature. Second Series. 3 vols. Cambridge, 1919–29.

Raby, F. J. E. A History of Secular Latin Poetry in the Middle Ages. Oxford, 1934.

Reese, Gustave. Music in the Middle Ages. New York, 1940.

Registrum de Dunfermelyn. Ed. C. Innes. Edinburgh, The Bannatyne Club, 1842.

Robb, T. D. The Thre Prestis of Peblis. Edinburgh, Scottish Text Society, 1920.

Robinson, F. N., ed. The Complete Works of Geoffrey Chaucer. Boston, 1933.

Rollins, H. E. "The Troilus-Cressida Story from Chaucer to Shakespeare," *Publications of the Modern Language Association,* XXXIII (1917), 383–429.

Root, R. K., ed. The Book of Troilus and Criseyde. Princeton, 1926.

Ross, W. D. Aristotle. London, 1923.

Rossetti, D. G. Dante and His Circle. London, 1874.

Roy, James A. "Of the Makaris: A Causerie," *University of Toronto Quarterly,* XVI (October, 1946), 30–41.

Saintsbury, George. History of English Prosody from the Twelfth Century to the Present Day. 3 vols. London, 1906–10.

—— A Short History of English Literature. New York, 1898.

Schick, J., ed. Lydgate's Temple of Glas. London, Early English Text Society, 1891.

Schweitzer, B. "Der bildende Künstler und der Begriff des Künstlerischen" *Neue Heidelberger Jahrbücher* (1925), pp. 28–132.

Shannon, E. F. Chaucer and the Roman Poets. Cambridge, 1929.

Sibbald, James, ed. Chronicle of Scottish Poetry. 4 vols. Edinburgh, 1802.

Sieper, Ernst, ed. Lydgate's Reson and Sensuallyte. London, Early English Text Society, 1901.

Simpson, J. Y. "Antiquarian Notices of Leprosy and Leper Hospitals in Scotland and England," *Edinburgh Medical and Surgical Journal,* 3 parts: LVI (1841), 301–330; LVII (1842), 121–56; 394–429.

Skeat, W. W., ed. The Complete Works of Geoffrey Chaucer. 6 vols. Oxford, 1894.

—— Chaucerian and Other Pieces (being a supplement to the Complete Works of Geoffrey Chaucer). Oxford, 1897.

—— The Kingis Quair: together with A Ballad of Good Counsel: by King James I of Scotland. London, 1911.

Small, John, ed. The Poetical Works of Gavin Douglas, Bishop of Dunkeld. 4 vols. Edinburgh, 1874.

Smith, G. Gregory. The Days of James IV. London, 1890.

—— ed. The Poems of Robert Henryson. 3 vols. Edinburgh and London, Scottish Text Society, 1906–14.

—— "The Scottish Chaucerians," Cambridge History of English Literature (New York, 1917), II, 272–303.

—— Scottish Literature Character and Influence. London, 1919.

—— ed. Specimens of Middle Scots. Edinburgh, 1902.

—— The Transition Period. London, 1927.

Smith, J. M. The French Background of Middle Scots Literature. Edinburgh, 1934.

Sommer, H. O., ed. The Recuyell of the Historyes of Troye. 2 vols. London, 1894.

Speirs, John. The Scots Literary Tradition. London, 1940.

Spurgeon, C. F. E. Five Hundred Years of Chaucer Criticism and Allusion. 3 vols. Cambridge, 1925.

Staveren, A. van, ed. Auctores Mythographi Latini. Leyden and Amsterdam, 1742.

Stearns, M. W. "Chaucer Mentions a Book," Modern Language Notes, LVII (January, 1942), 28–31.

—— A Modernization of Robert Henryson's Testament of Cresseid. Indiana University Publications, Humanity Series No. 13 (1945). Reprinted in Medieval English Verse and Prose, ed. R. S. Loomis and R. Willard, New York, 1948.

—— "A Note on Chaucer and Aristotelian Psychology," Studies in Philology, XLIII (January, 1946), 15–21.

—— "A Note on Chaucer's Attitude toward Love," Speculum, XVII (October, 1942), 570–74.

Steele, R., ed. Lydgate and Burgh's Secrees of Old Philisoffres. London, Early English Text Society, 1894.

Suter, H. "Die Mathematiker und Astronomen der Araber und ihre Werke," Abhandlungen zur Geschichte der Mathematischen Vol. X. Leipzig, 1910.

Sypherd, W. O. "Chaucer's Eight Years' Sickness," Modern Language Notes, XX (December, 1905), 240–43.

—— Studies in Chaucer's Hous of Fame. London, Chaucer Society, 1907.

Tatlock, J. S. P. "Astrology and Magic in Chaucer's *Franklin's Tale*," *Anniversary Papers* . . . *Kittredge* (Boston, 1913), pp. 339–50.

—— "The Epilog of Chaucer's *Troilus*," *Modern Philology,* XVIII (April, 1921), 113–47.

—— "The People in Chaucer's *Troilus*," *Publications of the Modern Language Association,* LVI (March, 1941), 85–104.

—— The Scene of the Franklin's Tale Visited. London, Chaucer Society, 1914.

Tawney, R. H. Religion and the Rise of Capitalism. London, 1926.

Taylor, James. The Pictorial History of Scotland. 2 vols. London, 1859.

Thomson, Daniel. The Weavers' Craft; Being a History of the Weavers' Incorporation of Dunfermline. Paisley, 1903.

Thulin, K. Die Götter des Martianus Capella und der Bronzeleber von Piacenza. Gieszen, 1906.

Tillotson, Geoffrey. Essays in Criticism and Research. Cambridge, 1942.

Tolkien, J. R. R., and E. V. Gordon, eds. Gawain and the Green Knight. Oxford, 1925.

Trevisano, Andrea. A Relation . . . of the Island of England . . . about the Year 1500. Tr. C. A. Sneyd. London, Camden Society, 1847.

Triggs, O. L., ed. The Assembly of Gods by John Lydgate. London, Early English Text Society, 1896.

Tuve, Rosemund. Seasons and Months: Studies in a Tradition of Middle English Poetry. Paris, 1933.

Veitch, John. The Feeling for Nature in Scottish Poetry. 2 vols. Edinburgh, 1887.

Vincent de Beauvais. Speculum Historiale. 3 vols. Augsburg, 1474.

—— Speculum Naturale. Strassburg, c. 1473.

Wageningen, I. van, ed. M. Manilii Astronomica. Leipzig, 1915.

Wallensis, Thomas. Metamorphosis Ouidiana Moraliter a Magistro Thoma vvaleys. Paris, 1515.

Ward, T. H. The English Poets. 5 vols. London, 1926.

Watt, L. M. Scottish Life and Poetry. London, 1912.

Webster, J. C. The Labors of the Months in Antique and Mediaeval Art to the End of the Twelfth Century. Princeton, 1938.

Wedel, T. O. The Mediaeval Attitude toward Astrology. New Haven, 1920.

West, C. B. Courtoisie in Anglo-Norman Literature. Oxford, 1938.

Whiting, B. J. "A Probable Allusion to Henryson's *Testament of Cresseid*," *Modern Language Review*, XL (January, 1945), 46–47.

Wickhoff, Franz. "Die Gestalt Amors in der Phantasie der italienischen Mittelalters," *Jahrbuch der Königlich Preussisichen Kunstsammlungen* (1890), XI, 41–53.

Wirl, Julius. Orpheus in der englischen Literatur. Vienna, 1913.

Wood, H. H., ed. The Poems and Fables of Robert Henryson. Edinburgh, 1933.

Wood, H. T. Chaucer's Influence on James I. Halle, 1879.

Wright, T. ed. Alexandri Neckham De Naturis Rerum Libri Duo. "Rolls Series." London, 1863.

Wülfing, J. E., ed. The Laud Troy Book. London, Early English Text Society, 1902.

Wüstenfeld, Ferdinand. "Die Übersetzungen arabischer Werke in das lateinische Seit dem XI. Jahrhundert," *Abhandlungen der Königlichen Gesellschaft der Wissenschaften zu Göttingen*, XXII (May, 1877), 1–53.

Young, K. "Chaucer's 'Troilus and Criseyde' as Romance," *Publications of the Modern Language Association*, LIII (1938), 37–63.

—— The Origin and Development of the *Story of Troilus and Criseyde*. London, Chaucer Society, 1908.

INDEX

Confessio Amantis (Gower), 60n
Confession and penance, 27 f., 114 f.
Contract-crime-punishment sequence, 54-60
Coulton, G. G., 5, 48n
Country and town living conditions contrasted, 33 ff., 109 ff.
Courtly love, attributes, 49; contrasting attitudes of Chaucer and Henryson toward, 53, 63-69; decline of complex ritual, 65
Court poets, Henryson not one, 6, 63, 124, 129
Courts, civil and ecclesiastical, 29; criticisms of, 29-32; fables in which criticized, 120, 123, 124 ff.
Covetousness, 32, 126, 127
Craftsmen and guilds, 35, 107
Creichton, Henry, 26
Cresseid, 48; parallels between character of Criseyde and, 52 ff.; *see also Testament of Cresseid*
Cynthia, described: qualities associated with, 46, 73, 95 f.

Dante, 103
De anima (Aristotle), 98
De Arte Honeste Amandi (Capellanus), 104
De Mundi Coelestis Terrestrisque . . . (Pseudo-Bede), 89; excerpt, 88
De Trinitate (Augustine) excerpt, 103
Dickins, Bruce, quoted, 86
Diet, *see* Food
Diomede, characterization of, 48
Dispossessed gentry, 107, 117
Douglas, Gawin, 6, 10; quoted, 9
Douglas, house of, 14, 15, 17n
Dove's Neck-Ring, 105
Dryden, John, 47
Dunbar, William, 3, 4, 6, 8; quoted, 9
Dunfermline, Abbot of, 26
Dunfermline, Henryson's designation as schoolmaster of, 10; reasons for which the royal burgh of, noted, 11; lepers, 43

Ecclesiastical courts and law, 29-32, 124 ff.
Economic background, *see* Socio-economic background
Edward IV of England, 15, 20n, 22, 24, 25
Elephantiasis, type of leprosy, 44n, 45, 46
England, wars with Scotland, 14, 15; question of loyalty to, 15; leprosy, 43
Erskine, Sir Thomas, 9
Evictions, *see* Land

Fables (Aesop), 107, 115; *see also Morall Fabillis of Esope*
Fables (Lydgate), 70
Fall of Princes, The (Lydgate), 58n, 60n
Fantasy, term, 100n
Farming and farm labor, 38 ff.; *see also* Land; Peasants
Feudalism, type of, 33; transition from, to a mercantile economy, 33, 42, 106, 129; why peasants harassed and evicted from land, 41 f., 117; landowners paradoxically hastening decline, by evictions, 106, 129
Feudal nobles, Henryson's outspoken and specific criticisms of, 17, 42, 106, 107, 117, 119, 126, 127, 128, 129
Fiametta (Boccaccio), 103
Filial ingratitude, 18 f., 25
Flodden, battle of, 15
Food, country fare, 35, 36; town, 37; dietary at Glasgow University, 37n
Foreign trade, 34, 35
Fortune, similarity between Love and, 90; described, 91 f.
Four horses of the Sun, 85 ff.; precedents for, *list*, 134 f.
Fox, the Wolf, and the Cadger, The, merchant class portrayed, 111 ff.
Fox, the Wolf, and the Husbandman, The, arguments re loyalty and legal procedure, 119 ff.
Fox, unusual characterization: logic, 114, 116
Fox and the Wolf, The, criticism of con-